FIGHT THE FEAR

Overcoming Obstacles That Stand In Your Way

Dr. Jeffrey L. Gurian

Happiness Center Publications
New York, New York

Cover Design by 100Covers.com
Interior Design by FormattedBooks.com

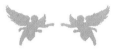

ABOUT THE AUTHOR

People often refer to Jeffrey Gurian as a "Renaissance Man" because he's involved in so many things. He's a former Cosmetic Dentist, and Clinical Prof. in Oral Medicine and Oro-Facial Pain at a major New York University, and a Board member of The Association for Spirituality and Psychotherapy, besides being a comedy writer, performer, director, author, producer, and radio personality, ... and not always in that order.

But it wasn't exactly easy for him to accomplish all those things. He's had to battle fear all along the way. Possibly inherited, or maybe internalized from an over-protective childhood, he never felt that the world was a safe place.

In his earlier book, "Healing Your Heart, By Changing Your Mind—A Spiritual and Humorous Approach To Achieving Happiness" which hit Best Seller status on Amazon, he explained how we all develop what he refers to as "heart wounds."

Starting from the time we're children, any time someone says something to hurt your feelings, or breaks a promise to you, or breaks up with you in a relationship, or hurts you in any way, we carry that energy inside of us in our heart chakras.

Basically we get "heart wounds" from unkind things that people have said to us, or from feelings of aloneness and "not being enough" that we develop for many possible reasons.

It could be caused by bullying, by discord in the home as a child, or sometimes it can even be from having learning disabilities that give us the idea that we're not as smart as other people, just because we process information in a different way.

This leads us into carrying negative messages about ourselves, which often translates into a negative worldview, confusion, and fear.

Jeffrey's own battles with what were diagnosed in later years as learning disabilities and a severe stutter, which started at age 6 or 7 and stayed with him throughout his 20's and beyond, gave him the impetus to stand up to his fears.

Through many years of hard work, he was able to develop a cure for his stuttering, and presently as an avocation he works with stutterers from all over the world, to teach them how not to stutter.

He's learned to confront his fears on a daily basis, still not completely understanding the cause of them, but understanding that they would be very happy if he never accomplished anything and just stayed at home, in bed, under the covers where it always feels safe.

As a Board member of The Association for Spirituality and Psychotherapy since 1999, he's come to learn that millions of people experience fear as well, and that it often keeps them from achieving their goals.

Fear is a bully that needs to be stood up to and confronted, so that like most bullies it just slinks away. That is the reason he wrote this book. It's a sequel to his previous book that teaches people to examine their thoughts, to see which thoughts they're holding about themselves that aren't valid.

It's not an easy thing to examine your thoughts objectively, because we tend to believe all our thoughts. The important fact to remember is that we created all of our thoughts, and those thoughts are not necessarily based on our experience, but on our INTERPRETATION of our experience, which can be two very different things.

It's the reason why two children can grow up in the same household, with the same parents and be two completely different people. And if you asked them about their childhood, you might think they grew up in two different homes.

The other important fact to remember is that any thought you create, you can also un-create, which is how he cured himself of stuttering by convincing his sub-conscious mind that he no longer "needed" to stutter. There was really nothing wrong with him. He created a "false disability" for himself.

In this book we learn how to convince our sub-conscious minds that there's really nothing to be afraid of by incorporating both a cognitive and Spiritual approach, with the understanding that "Fear is the Opposite of Faith", and that if your faith is strong there is no room in your life for fear.

Certain fear is reasonable of course, like fear of sky-diving or engaging in a sport where there is the chance of being hurt, but the fear we're talking about is the fear that tells you that you can't accomplish your goals, because of something about yourself that isn't really true.

The author is an expert in fighting against fear, and challenges himself all the time with things like a solo two-week trip to Japan, just because traveling is so difficult for him, and brings up every fear he could imagine.

His success in fighting the fear has allowed him to work, and perform in the comedy world with legends like Rodney Dangerfield, Joan Rivers, George Wallace, Phil Hartman, Richard Belzer, Gilbert Gottfried, Jerry Lewis, and Andrew "Dice" Clay, among many others.

And for those of you old enough to remember, he even worked with Mr. Television, Milton Berle who was Jeffrey's sponsor in the legendary Friars Club.

Jeffrey has performed at most of the big clubs in N.Y. and L.A. and was featured several times on Comedy Central's hit Kroll Show with Nick Kroll, John Mulaney, Amy Poehler, Seth Rogen, Laura Dern and Katy Perry.

He was actually the first to be pranked with Too Much Tuna in the viral "Too Much Tuna" sketch on Kroll Show, and was also a regular on-air personality on Sirius XM's Bennington Show, (formerly Ron and Fez), for two years, where he also brought on special guests/friends like Russell Peters, Trevor Noah, Colin Quinn, Artie Lange, Susie Essman, D.L. Hughley, and Lisa Lampanelli.

He's also a comedy journalist and has been covering the comedy scene since 1999. From 2014-2019 he wrote a weekly column covering the comedy scene for The Interrobang called "Jumping Around With Jeffrey Gurian", and has also written for MTV, National Lampoon, Weekly World News, The Weekly Humorist and many Friars Roasts.

His Comedy Matters TV You Tube channel has over 500 A-list celebrity interviews including Jimmy Fallon, Judd Apatow, Marc Maron, Bill Burr, Tracy Morgan, Chelsea Handler, Jim Carrey, Trevor Noah, Lisa Lampanelli, Susie Essman, Nick Kroll, Amy Schumer, Gilbert Gottfried, John Mulaney, Amy Poehler, and many, many more, with well over two million views.

He's produced shows starring Kevin Hart and Susie Essman, and according to Paul Provenza and Nick Kroll is known by everyone in comedy. Nick says on camera that "nobody has more access to people in comedy than Jeffrey Gurian."

He filmed several episodes of Real Housewives of New York, in which he created a sketch for

Countess LuAnn and Princess Carole Radziwill. He also recently filmed an episode of Crashing at the request of director Judd Apatow.

Two of his greatest accomplishments discussed in detail in this book were surviving a "widow-maker" heart attack in 2015, and surviving a hospitalization in March of 2020 with Covid Double Pneumonia.

This is his 7th book. His last book "Healing Your Heart, By Changing Your Mind—A Spiritual and Humorous Approach To Achieving Happiness" is available as an e-book, a paperback and an audio book. This is the link to the book:
https://tinyurl.com/yx8h3mw7

He hopes you enjoy this book and go on to "Fight the Fear" in your own lives!

If you'd like to be on Jeffrey's mailing list please send an e-mail to Jeffrey@jeffreygurian.com. For more on Jeffrey, to sign up for his mailing list, and to receive a free gift please visit:

https://mailchi.mp/jeffreygurian/healingyourheart

And please subscribe to his Comedy Matters TV channel on You Tube at
https://www.youtube.com/comedymatterstv

On Twitter and IG he's @jeffreygurian

EDITORIAL REVIEWS

"Fight the Fear", by Jeffrey Gurian is the author's latest contribution to the inspirational self-help field. The author, a fellow therapist, comedian, former Cosmetic Dentist, and Professor, carefully explains how to fight fear and achieve your goals. This book chronicles his own battles with fear, stuttering, ADHD, traveling, self-limiting thinking, and professional challenges, and even his two close brushes with death including a serious heart attack, and Covid double pneumonia. Through inner strength and determination he manages to overcome them all, pushing himself through each challenge, and in sharing with us how he did it, inspires us to do the same. This is an important book!

Sam Menahem Ph.D.
Author of "The Great Cosmic Lesson Plan: Healing through Spirituality, Humor and Music;

Past Pres. of the Assoc. for Spirituality and Psychotherapy.

The only thing I ever feared was going to the dentist and Jeffrey cured me of that! Read this book!

Curtis Sliwa,
WABC Radio Host,
Founder of The Guardian Angels,
next Mayor of NYC

"We've all been held back in life by fear, which can manifest itself in many forms—self-sabotage, confusion, procrastination, and fear of success, to name a few. Jeffrey Gurian knows what it's like and bravely shares how he battled his own fears to become a doctor, best-selling author, comedy writer for big stars, performer, radio personality, and even more—he even overcame a severe stutter by developing his own cure!

You, too, can overcome any fear to achieve your goals. Gurian's brave and honest plan will show you the way. Bravo, Jeffrey, for helping so many overcome so much.

FIGHT THE FEAR and change your life!"

Judith Regan,
President & Publisher, Regan Arts

"Jeffrey Gurian is a living landmark. Anyone remotely connected to the world of comedy knows and loves Jeffrey as a guy who loves comedy and loves life even more. It's a testament to him that I had no idea that he faces down deep-seated fears daily. We should all learn to appreciate our lives the way Jeffrey does his, and this book is a great way to start."

Evan Shapiro,
Pres. of National Lampoon

"The very first time I walked into Jeffrey Gurian's apartment I noticed the pictures that covered the walls, and covered his decades of work in the comedy world. The second thing I noticed was the balloons. They were everywhere, and when I asked him "why" he said they were a symbol of Happiness.

That said it all to me! This man gets life, and understands human behavior. As I got to know Jeffrey, I began to understand how he got to this place of peace…despite feeling FEAR. He embodies the saying, "Courage is not a lack of fear, it's feeling the fear and doing it anyway." Jeffrey's really figured it all out…and is now sharing the secret...Thank you Jeffrey!"

Tim Sabean (aka Creator of the
Howard Stern Channels)
Chief Content Officer of React.Net

"It is hard to believe that such a sensitive and empathic person could face the harshness of this world and not only survive, but thrive. The importance of this book is in sharing the courage it takes to overcome the obstacles that might keep you from fulfilling your greatest dreams.

But for Jeffrey Gurian the world is a dangerous place. As Mark Twain said: "I've had a lot of worries in my life, most of which never happened." With Jeffrey they do happen.... Each moment is a potential disaster. Jeffrey explains why: Total and complete self-sabotage. You tend to manifest your worst fears. Even if you're aware of it and can diagnose it, it still doesn't mean you won't engage in it. It's a constant battle, but you can never stop fighting.

It's not easy to be Jeffrey. He's possessed with an excess amount of fear and worry complicated by a string of an alphabet of afflictions: ADHD, ADD, OCD. But it is also wonderful to be Jeffrey too—grateful, kind and the ability to laugh at himself.

For someone riddled with adversities, if he didn't have the courage to solve those riddles, the world would surely have missed some of the funniest lines from people he wrote jokes for: Jerry Lewis, Joan Rivers, Rodney Dangerfield, among many others.

He has not allowed fear to make a difference in his life, thanks to his resolve and an overwhelming desire to succeed in spite of himself. He knows he is here to follow his dreams and become all he can be. Jeffrey is an outstanding example of someone who meets life's challenges with extreme courage while shaking all the way.

He knows how to tread on difficult paths in order to arrive at the desired goal. When he says: "Everything makes me uncomfortable." We know he is not exaggerating, he is just showing up for another test of self-assertion. Lacking all self-pity and with audacious determination, such as getting through the stage door to meet his idol Woody Allen, Jeffrey conquers himself despite all obstacles.

While most people meet some days full of slight inconveniences, for Jeffrey it feels like a daily struggle of life and death situations, or so it appears to him. He must constantly do battle with the demons of self-sabotage, lack of self worth, and worries that try to keep him stuck. In each moment of engagement with the forces that bind him, he must find the inexhaustible strength to free himself.

It could be excruciatingly painful to be Jeffrey, but it must also be wonderfully pleasant, full of love, joy, wonder and laughter. Jeffrey's teaching is the guide to others: "Go against uncomfortability to ask for help, beacause when you're all alone, if you don't advocate for yourself, no one else can or will....

In this book Jeffrey takes the reader on a series of Quixote-esque adventures. He says: "Because I believe in confronting my fears, which is the only way to make them disappear, I decided to go to Europe alone for two weeks.

Oy, not a trip you want to be on with Jeffrey, because when he travels he needs one extra suitcase just to take his fears along with him. Simple fears: "Fear I'll be hungry and have nothing to eat, or thirsty and have nothing to drink, or have to use the bathroom in an awkward situation, and these fears still reside in the back of my mind."

"There's fears of being late, missing my connection, which I don't think has ever happened, and unexpected things like that. But the point is I never let it stop me. I just go. And so should YOU!"

So sometimes we have to laugh with Jeffrey... and sometimes at him: "Just once I'd like to travel without hearing someone yell out, 'Excuse me sir, does this belong to you?' " Nevertheless, thanks to the kindness of strangers, Jeffrey lives in a world of miraculous encounters.

"Nowhere during any of my travels did I see one other person whose luggage kept tipping over, and falling all over the ground. No one travels with the lack of grace that I travel with, and it's all through no fault of my own. I manifest it through my fears." But the lack of grace is Jeffrey's grace. Although he travels under a dark cloud of his own making, the sky is always open for him to fill him with sunshine and surprises.

Another example of his courage was one of his earliest confrontations with himself. Take his childhood stuttering. What would have stopped most people from being in the public eye propelled Jeffrey to learn and conquer. But again, he knew what he wanted. He proclaimed to himself and the world: "It's very hard to make your way in this world when you can't communicate. Especially if you want to be a doctor, or a performer. Unfortunately for me, I wanted to do both! Talk about making your life complicated!"

It was not just effective communication that Jeffrey discovered for his success, it was the extra bonus of "learning to control your mind."

Read this book at the risk of changing your life and seeking out the places you need to conquer. Witness the exquisite details of this Mensch-making man, always appreciative for the help with a kind word and a sweet sentiment for all, who says: *"Fortunately, I have learned not to accept the fear that my subconscious mind creates…."*

And although he is constantly dodging the mine field of the outer world and the mind fields of the inner world, Jeffrey doesn't walk through circumstances, he floats with luck and good fortune, guiding him onwards.

Somehow in fighting the fear he always seems to land on his feet and be the better for it. And as the reader making your way through the adventures of one man's challenging dance through life—you might be inspired to learn how to control your mind, conquer your fears and live in the joyful possibility of fulfilling your dreams. Because if Jeffrey can, he feels you can too.

Alan Steinfeld,
founder of New Realities

TABLE OF CONTENTS

DEDICATION

I want to dedicate this book to my wonderful parents Marjorie and Raymond Gurian, two of the most loving and supportive parents anyone could ask for, who unfortunately and accidentally gave me every fear known to man.

I was never taught that the world was a safe place. I grew up with the feeling that something bad could happen to me at any given moment. I was over-protected and kept in a crib until I was 6 ½ years old. (Really!) I will go into that more inside the book but suffice it to say I that if I had a tattoo, which I don't, it wouldn't say "Born To Be Wild", it would say "Born To Be Nervous!"

My father grew up without a Dad. His Dad left when he was very young which was not common in those days. He was raised by a single Mom, and so was not able to afford to go to medical school, which had been his dream.

Instead he became a liquor salesman, which he did successfully for 40 years. He worked so hard, night and day, and didn't get much out of it because his company didn't treat the salesmen too well. Growing up he was my hero, and I wanted to be just like him, and follow in his footsteps, which he wouldn't allow.

Everyone who ever met him liked my Dad. He was such a great guy with a great sense of humor. Always looking for the laugh. He often helped newcomers to the field open their own liquor stores, and many times I asked I him why he never opened his own store, and he always had a reason, but the real reason was fear.

No one ever taught him how to do anything like that growing up. His Mom, my wonderful Nana Kitty worked in a dry cleaning store, and literally once walked a very long distance to return a quarter that she found in someone's jacket.

He had no one to guide him, and so when I graduated from college and went on to become a dentist it was his greatest honor. I was the first in my family to become a professional. Both of my parents were so proud of me, but I inherited the fear that ran in the family.

I've been fighting it all my life and if you are reading this book, I assume you have been too.

I want to add a special dedication to my sister Ronnie who has also been battling fear her whole life, and accomplished many wonderful things in spite of it. She's truly an inspiration, and I hope she knows that!

I'm very grateful that both of my daughters Elizabeth and Kathryn turned out to be fearless adults. They take on life as it comes, and they do it with ease and grace.

And as a final thought, because I'm a big believer in synchronicity, on the very day I was writing this page, I opened my local newspaper to the Horoscope section, ... just because, ... I looked under Capricorn, and this is what it said, "A fear of some kind has held you back long enough. Now you must find your courage and push past it. Don't worry that others might think you are being selfish or pushy—worry only that if you don't take the action the fear may never go away."

I swear that it happened just that way on the very day I wrote this, and I take that as a sign from above that I'm meant to write this book, and hopefully to help many people living with FEAR!

INTRODUCTION

We all face fear to some degree, but how we handle it differs from person to person. Sometimes the fear comes from personal experience, and other times just from our thoughts. Either way it can be just as damaging.

Many of us create our fears. Some of us are just born that way. The word "fearful" means full of fear, and was a very good description of me.

In the powerful and Spiritual 12 step programs they talk a lot about fear. Fear can drive you to drink and take drugs. In their literature they even talk about experiencing "a hundred forms of fear."

I've been confronting fear all my life. For whatever reason, fear told me I'd never have the things other people had. Why I don't know. My parents couldn't have been more loving and supportive.

I believe in the Collective Consciousness so I may have inherited the fear of my ancestors passed down from generation to generation. I may have inherited the fear from The Holocaust which I heard about as a young child.

Why I had the fear is not as important as how I deal with it. Present tense. I feel like I confront my fear on a daily basis. So many things make me uncomfortable.

The way I think of it is if the rest of the world seems to be able to do a certain thing comfortably, I have to be able to do it as well.

And I'm not talking about potentially dangerous things like skydiving or extreme skiing, I'm talking about things like traveling, or making a simple phone call to someone who's expecting your call, or going onstage to perform.

That last example would probably strike fear into most people, but not if you want to be an entertainer!

Fear is a bully. One of the best sayings I ever heard is that "Courage is not a lack of fear. Courage is having the fear and doing it anyway."

That rings true for me. In the pages of this book I will discuss my own fear in various areas of my life, and how I had to overcome it in order to achieve the things in my life I was able to achieve.

My fear told me I would never have a profession, or a home, or a wife or a family. It told me I would never be successful. Fortunately I was able to attain all those things and more, but I didn't do it comfortably. I did them all while experiencing fear.

Hopefully you will relate to and identify with some of the things I say and it will help you to overcome your own fears. Knowledge is power!

By the way, you'll notice that certain words like Happiness are written with a capital letter, which is usually reserved only for proper names. I take the liberty of capitalizing any word I feel is important enough to deserve the honor. It's like giving respect to the word, so I thank you in advance for indulging me! (LOL)

I also start a lot of sentences with the word "But"! I know you're not supposed to, but I write the way I speak, and if you comment on that I'll know you didn't read my whole "Introduction!"

With my wonderful family!

CHAPTER

1

The Essence Of Fear

FEAR is a four-letter word. F-E-A-R . Some people think of these four letters as standing for "F" Everything And Run! I prefer to think of them as standing for "False Evidence Appearing Real", or "Face Everything And Recover."

Fear is a bully. It doesn't want you to accomplish anything. It wants you to stay home in bed with the covers over your head. Fortunately bullies usually back down when you stand up to them.

I've been fighting fear since I was a child. As I stated previously, I guess I was never taught that the world was a safe place. Not that it is, ... but some people are taught to feel secure growing up. I must have missed that lesson because I was a mass of fears.

A lot of it was from being over-protected as a child. As I mentioned in the dedication, my mother kept me in a crib until I was 6 ½ years old. I'm not kidding. Six and a half years old. I have a very clear memory of my grandfather bringing me my first two-wheeler bike, and I climbed out of my crib to see it.

I think they kept the training wheels on for years! In later years I asked her why she kept me in a crib so long, and the reason I was given was that it was for space.

They were waiting for me to have a sibling. Thank G-d my sister was finally born when I was 6 ½ or else who knows how long I would have stayed in that crib.

That probably accounted for some of the fear. I think another factor was that I feel I internalized fear from the Collective Consciousness of The Holocaust. The fact that millions of people could be killed for something they believed in was incredibly disturbing to me even as a child. I was a very sensitive child way before I learned to own that sensitivity as a gift and not as a burden.

There was a Holocaust survivor living in my neighborhood, a little boy named Ziggy who became a friend of mine.

I remember the first day I met him. He was wearing a royal blue coat with a matching peaked cap, and the people in the neighborhood used to whisper about how his parents survived, and escaped to this country. I think they called him a "displaced person." That made me nervous. What kind of person is "displaced?"

Then in another building across the street from me was my friend Walter who came from a strict German family, and everyone whispered about them as well. His father was the super of the building and I think that everyone wondered if he was a Nazi. That too made me nervous.

It's funny but I don't recall if Ziggy and Walter played together. They only lived a block apart and it would have been interesting if they did.

But everything made me nervous as a kid. I recall very clearly being afraid of the dark. And it bothered me a lot that I was afraid of the dark. I had a lot of nightmares as a kid. Some were recurrent and I didn't like to go to sleep, which is a trait I carry to this day, but not for the same reason.

In those days it was because I had so many fears. These days if it involves fear at all, it's the fear of losing time. If you sleep eight hours a night you may be healthy but you've slept away a full third of your life. That's too much sleep for me, and too much time to waste.

But even as I child I confronted my fears. I don't know how I did it, or where I got the courage, but I was so scared of the dark that it was incapacitating to me. So somehow, I made myself walk into my bedroom at night in the dark.

It was pitch black and I was shaking. I remember walking in the dark and looking under my cover, under my bed, and in my closet to assure myself that there was no real reason to be afraid. I just kept doing that until the fear left me.

I also had recurrent nightmares. I used to dream that two scary looking men with weird names and very long fingernails would come into my room at night and try to wake me up by running their long nails against my skin.

Another of my recurring nightmares had to do with one of my grandmothers. I had two very loving and devoted grandmothers. One lived next door to me in The Bronx where I grew up. That was my mother's mother.

The other, my father's mother, lived in another section of The Bronx and came to visit occasionally where she might babysit for me if my parents went out. She was widowed and worked in a dry cleaning store during the day.

She couldn't have been more kind and loving. In the basement of my building, which always scared me, there was a laundry room, and then there were huge pipes and a boiler room right near the elevator.

I used to glance in there and the boiler room really made me nervous. It had huge machines in there that made a lot of noise and I found it to be very scary. I can still picture it today thanks to cellular memory.

My recurrent nightmare was that my grandmother would take me down there and then leave me there alone. I dreamt that night after night and it disturbed me so much that I finally did something I was told was very unusual, and it was the first time I actually remember learning to control my mind.

In the middle of the dream, I turned to my grandmother and said to her, "You're not my grandmother, this is just a dream!" I remember doing that so clearly.

Psychiatrists have told me that this is a very rare thing for a child to be able to do, ... to comprehend during the dream that it's a dream, and to be able to control your mind to that degree to acknowledge that within the dream.

And as I recall the bad dreams stopped after that. But the fear didn't.

I had a bad case of ADD (Attention Deficit Disorder) but they didn't know what that was in those days. It causes a lot of confusion which for me leads to fear.

I must have also had a bit of OCD because I distinctly recall that if I was walking in the school hallway and accidentally brushed my left leg against something I had to brush my right leg against something in order to feel even.

I also developed a stuttering problem when I was about 6 or 7 years old, which followed me well into my 20's and beyond. I stuttered and blocked on words, which made my life very difficult.

Traumas are deeply engrained in our consciousness, and I recall a time in junior high school when I was called on by the teacher to answer a question. In those days when you answered a question in school you had to stand next to your seat and address the class.

I stood up to answer but literally nothing came out. I tried, but literally not a sound came out and

I just stood there turning red, until I finally just sat down. It felt like an eternity but was probably just a couple of minutes.

I played the piano and took lessons from when I was 7 until I was 17. I was a very sensitive child, which I'll get into later, and was also trained to be a perfectionist. If I couldn't do something perfectly I didn't want to do it at all.

I remember playing the piano at a recital of some kind in elementary school. It was in a big auditorium packed with people. I recall that my parents were there. I was very afraid that I would make a mistake.

I sat at the piano and began to play but at some point I did make a mistake and as I recall I stopped playing and got up and left the piano. Right in the middle of the performance! Thinking about that now is still uncomfortable to me. I wish I remembered what happened afterwards. My Dad probably took me out for a hamburger.

Whenever there was a parent/teacher conference, no matter what kind of report I got my Dad would always bring me home a hamburger. I didn't remember that until I was writing this paragraph, but it's a nice memory.

But the point is I was always riddled with fear. In high school my stuttering was so bad and I was so afraid to speak in class that I signed up for a speech class. Not a speech therapy class but a class where you had to give speeches.

I don't know how I found the courage to do that but despite my fears I was always determined to beat them. Amazingly when it was my turn to give a speech I never stuttered. The other kids couldn't believe it. I myself couldn't believe it.

What I came to figure out was that when I got up there to speak I became someone else. I became the Jeffrey that didn't stutter.

Almost like an actor takes on a role in a movie script. I allowed myself to become someone else, because my subconscious mind, which is the part of my mind that decided that I needed to stutter, only demanded that I personally needed to stutter. Me! The Jeffrey Gurian that it recognized.

If I allowed myself to become someone else, my sub-conscious mind did not recognize that person as me, and had no need to make that person stutter.

As an avocation I work with stutterers and one of the exercises I do with them is to have them speak in a different made-up voice. It could be a crazy cartoon voice, or a deeper voice, or a higher voice, as long as it's not the voice that their subconscious mind is used to hearing. Invariably their speech becomes much better.

I would emphasize that I only have them do that as an exercise to prove to them how their mind works. The goal is for them to speak the way everyone else does who doesn't stutter, and in a voice that is their true voice.

Unfortunately you can't go through life speaking in a bizarre voice just so you don't stutter, but it shows them how the subconscious mind works and gives them the confidence to know that there's really nothing wrong with them and that they can conquer stuttering because it's all in the mind. It has to do with your thoughts, and also a lot about self-sabotage.

When I went to college I made myself run for the President of the Freshman class. I went to a very big city school, which was fed in by 7 different high schools. I only knew the kids from my own high school, and could never say my own name without stuttering. The hard "G" in Gurian was impossible for me to say.

Most stutterers have a hard time saying their names and that is not a coincidence. My feeling is that your name is your identity and if you're not happy with who you are then you don't feel comfortable telling your name to people, so you stutter and block on it.

I made myself run for election telling myself that if I won the election I wouldn't have to stutter anymore because it would show me that people liked me. You can't win an election if no one votes for you. I guess I had a feeling that it had to do with how I felt about myself and how I thought people felt about me.

And that's strange too because in high school which is a weird time for most people, I was voted one of the "Senior Celebrities", which was basically a popularity contest. They did that in those days. "Prettiest Girl", "Handsomest Guy", "Most Popular". I was voted "Most Talented" in the yearbook because I played the piano and drums and I could sing as well. The truth was it was strictly a popularity contest.

But I never felt like I fit in. I was two years younger than everyone else because I had skipped two grades, and was physically much smaller than most of the other kids as well.

To avoid having to say my name I had other students act as my campaign managers to introduce me to students I didn't know, and they would ask them to vote for me. Once I got started speaking I could get some words out but it helped to have other kids introduce me.

I ran against a guy named Steve who thought he was a big-shot. He was really obnoxious and said some very mean things about me so I decided to teach him a lesson by playing a trick on him.

I went to a big school party where he was at and brought my best friend Kenny who didn't even go to the school. I sent Kenny over to introduce himself to Steve and tell him that he heard he was running for President and that he wanted to back him in the election.

Kenny was supposedly from a big school and knew a lot of people and could get Steve a lot of votes. At least that's what he told Steve. As they were becoming BFF's I "just happened" to walk by.

Kenny calls me over and we exchange big hugs and he says, "Hey Jeff great to see you. I want you to meet Steve. He's running for Freshman President and we should back him!"

To which I said, "Hey man, I'm the guy who's running against him!" To which Kenny then said to Steve, "Oh man, I'm so sorry. I can't back someone against my good friend Jeffrey. I have to give all my votes to him. Sorry man!" And Steve turned white!

Anyway I won the election, and it was a great lesson for me. I was the President of the Freshman Class of hundreds of kids and I still stuttered, and it taught me that outside validation doesn't work. It doesn't matter how many people tell you you're wonderful and talented and amazing, it matters what you think of yourself. It's an inside job.

I took that information and began my quest to rid myself of the burden of stuttering. It took many years of hard work until I was successful.

When I was only 12 years old I decided that I wanted to be a dentist. I was also already writing comedy. The thought of doing those two diverse things confused me even then.

I knew I wanted to be some kind of a doctor, but my sensitivity told me that I could never handle life and death situations, and I liked going to my orthodontist so that's what I decided to be.

In my senior year of college I applied for dental schools with great trepidation. Somewhere along the line I had decided that I wasn't meant to have the things that most people take for granted. I thought I would never have my own apartment, never have a business, or get married or have a family.

Why I had such negative thoughts about myself I'm not sure, but somewhere I got the idea that I wasn't enough. Very often these thoughts come from remarks made by other kids, bullies, or even strangers who comment on you because they think they can.

Part of the exam to be admitted to dental school in those days involved having to carve a piece of chalk with a knife. The talk was that it was a very difficult thing to do and that if you broke your chalk you'd fail automatically and could not go to dental school. Welcome lots of fear!

I remember taking the dental school entrance exams, which I think was at least a two-day test, and when they gave out the chalk they gave you two pieces. You had to carve exact shapes into both pieces within a certain amount of time, and they had to be exact to the millimeter according to measurements the instructors provided.

There were tricks like blowing on your chalk to moisten it with your breath so it wouldn't crack too easily. Some kids knew tricks that other kids didn't know. It was already very cutthroat.

I recall not having started on my second piece of chalk when they warned us that time was almost up. I raced through my second piece and was sure I had failed the test.

I remember the excitement I felt the day my mother got the mail and gave me a letter of acceptance to Temple University School of Dentistry. I had been accepted into two other schools as well.

One was Buffalo, which I declined because I thought the weather was too cold, and that I would be depressed and have a hard time studying. I had gone up there with my Dad for the interview and coming home we were chased down the highway by a snowstorm.

The other school was in Maryland, which was the very first dental school in the country, but I decided to go to Philadelphia because it was close to New York and I had never been away from home before. Not even sleep away camp.

I only went to day camp. I had never even been on an airplane. People in the Bronx didn't really travel anywhere in those days.

It was a big thing to drive to Florida with your family which we did a couple of times. My Dad would make sure we got up at the crack of dawn or even before that to get on the road very early.

I think that started me getting nervous about traveling and packing. Something about having to get up early, and pack and then getting my suitcases to my car makes me nervous to this day. I fumble and forget a million things.

As a matter of fact when my first daughter was an infant, and we were going up to our country home, I packed the car and left the suitcase with all the baby clothes on the sidewalk and drove away. That is a manifestation of nervousness and fear.

Luckily a little girl from the neighborhood found the suitcase and thought they were doll's clothes and brought them to her mother who managed to return them to us.

I also think that's why when I fly I look for afternoon flights so I don't have to get up super early to get ready, and worry about getting stuck in rush hour traffic and possibly missing my flight.

I recently confronted my fear of traveling, and went to Japan alone for two weeks. Talk about confronting fear of traveling!

I had to start packing about a week before my trip to make sure I didn't engage in self-sabotage and forget everything that's important to me. The concept of self-sabotage will also be discussed later in the book.

My Dad and my cousin Stanley helped me move down to Philadelphia into a little apartment in a very bad neighborhood in North Philadelphia. I think the purpose of having professional schools in poor neighborhoods is so they could have lots of patients for the clinic. I think a lot of professional schools are purposely put in bad neighborhoods for that reason. Rich people tend not to go to clinics.

But this was really bad. There were killings there. I often describe it as being so bad that youth gangs were afraid to go there. They had to bring another gang with them to feel safe! (LOL)

That element of danger alone caused me to have a lot of fear. If you didn't have enough food you couldn't go out alone at night to shop. It wasn't safe enough. You had to wait for the next day.

The very first day of school the Dean made what was supposed to be a welcoming speech, but it wasn't very welcoming. I recall his exact words, which are forever etched into my consciousness.

He said, "We don't want any free thinkers here. If you want to be a hippy with a guitar, go to dental school in California!" That set the stage for what would become the worst four years of my life. That will be a separate chapter in the book.

Suffice it to say in this introductory chapter that I went on to attain all the things I thought I would never get. I had a big successful dental practice and was a leader in Cosmetic Dentistry, which was a new thing when I graduated.

I met a great girl and got married. I had an apartment and then a big house in the suburbs, and had two beautiful daughters, and was scared at every moment.

It took me a while to learn that there are only two basic fears in life, fear of losing what you have and fear of not getting what you want.

Fear and trauma are deeply engrained into our consciousness thanks to something called "Cellular Memory" which to me is a fascinating topic. It simply means that every single thing you ever experienced in all of your senses since you were born is still inside of you affecting everything you do and every thought you have.

It's the reason you can hear a song you like and it will remind you of the boy or girl you liked in the fifth grade, or the reason you can get a whiff of some perfume and it will take you all the way back to your kindergarten teacher who wore that perfume and carried that scent.

It's like a sensory déjà vu! And the traumatic events are the ones that are the most deeply engrained. Those are the ones I call "heart wounds" that are the topic of my last book on Happiness called, "Healing Your Heart, By Changing Your Mind—A Spiritual and Humorous Approach To Achieving Happiness."

Those "heart wounds" affect our self-esteem and self-confidence and every decision we make or don't make, which is why they need to be released. They are very much connected to Fear!

And as you learn more about Fear, you'll see as I mentioned previously, that most fears fall into two categories, the fear of losing what you have and the fear of not getting what you want. Think about it and you'll see that it's true.

The rest of this book will take you through all the fears I faced, how I learned to get past them and how I learned to stand up to the bully known as FEAR!

You may also notice that I repeat certain things throughout the book. I'm vey aware of that and I do it purposely. Nobody learns anything by hearing it once. It's only through repetition that we learn.

CHAPTER

2

The Nightmare Of Dental School

My four years in dental school were probably the worst four years of my life. And I don't say that facetiously. I wouldn't be surprised if my experiences in dental school were still affecting me in some way today.

The way I look at it, we should have been welcomed into the school by doctors who were happy that we wanted to join their profession. It should have felt like an honor to be accepted in dental school, and it did until I got there.

I was very excited to be able to become a doctor, but to my great surprise it wasn't a welcoming experience at all.

Instead it turned into a four-year fraternity hazing. It was almost how they portray the Marines where the drill sergeant screams at the troops for the smallest infraction.

In dental school if they addressed you as "Dr." you knew you were in trouble. "Ok Dr., come up to the blackboard!"

I really thought the doctors who taught there would be supportive and glad that we were joining them in their field.

The problem was and still is to a great extent that many men treat each other very poorly in the concept of "making a man out of you." They often call it "busting balls." I HATE that!

I liken it to a kind of "jock mentality" where you're only considered cool if you excel at sports, or can talk non-stop ABOUT sports, and/or if you can chug beers and don't particularly care about your appearance, or have any style or fashion sense, except for maybe a backwards baseball cap.

So the very first day of school when the Dean made that so-called "welcoming" speech and told us that if we wanted to be free thinkers we should go to dental school in California the stage was set for what was to come.

Almost immediately I began getting picked on because of my hair which was not particularly long at all. As a matter of fact it was short, but they didn't like the style.

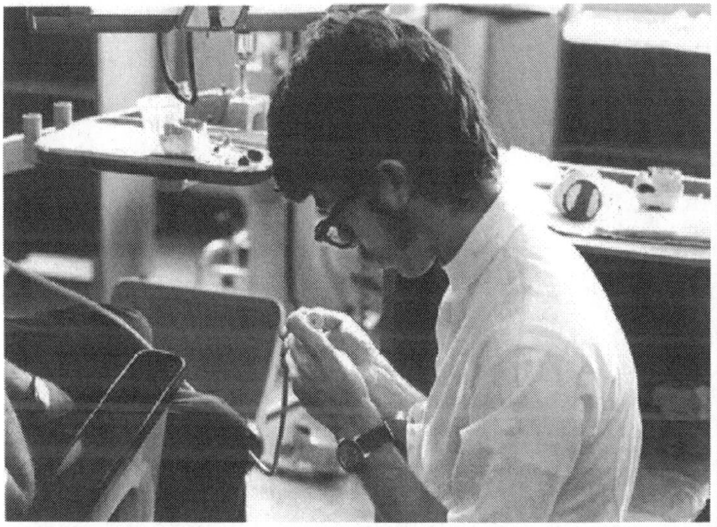

This is the hair length that got me banned from seeing patients for three weeks, and told I was a "disgrace" to the profession.

Plus I made the cardinal mistake at one point of growing a moustache. To the powers that be, that was the equivalent of being a heroin addict.

Well in those days in Philadelphia if you wore a turtleneck sweater you might as well have been one of the Weathermen. (A radical political group!) You were immediately branded as a radical.

For some unknown reason I was immediately branded as an outcast, not only by the instructors but by the students as well. I wasn't used to that as I had always had tons of friends and was very social.

Friends were important to have in dental school because the workload was so heavy that people had to work in groups. That need was especially important for the course called gross anatomy where you dissect the human body. It's too much work to do alone. And it's aptly named because when you first start out it's kind of gross!

The very first day when they handed out the bodies, none of us had ever seen a dead body before. They were in plastic bags, which we had to cut off and remove. The bodies didn't look human. They had been injected with formaldehyde and looked very pale and gray. All I remember was that we started dissecting the body in the armpit, to see a plexus of nerves.

Students broke up into study groups, and split up the work among four or five guys, (there was only one woman in the class), and they would share the burden of the research and even test each other to make sure they were making progress. I wound up working alone.

Most of the guys were heavy beer drinkers, and played baseball on teams they created, and I was left out of both of those things, mainly because I didn't do them. It wasn't my style. New York was a very different place than Philly in those days, ... the 1970's.

It was soon after "The Summer of Love" and Woodstock and I was all in. I was at Woodstock with a few friends on our way to Montreal the night before the music started. When we woke up to heavy rain we decided to leave and continue on to Montreal.

If we hadn't we would probably still be there! (LOL) There were a half a million kids from all over the country and I was probably the only one of all those half a million kids who wanted to be a dentist.

Anyway I was insulted and humiliated in dental school almost on a daily basis. There were two instructors who were the worst to me. I won't mention their names because I don't want their energy in this book, but a recent meeting with the current Dean of that very same dental school confirmed my worst thoughts about them.

They were both racists and anti-Semites. This new Dean admitted as much to me. One had a Confederate flag in his office and a flag that said

"The South Will Rise Again." He had the kind of crew cut that looked like his hair had been dug out with a shovel.

The other torturer was Pennsylvania Dutch, also with a crew cut and thin wire glasses and was an exact double for an SS officer in the Third Reich. I can still picture his red, angry face today.

And these men ran the two most important departments in which you needed a certain amount of experience and a certain amount of credits in order to graduate.

The first year of school we had one project and that was to make a set of dentures from scratch. We had one year to do the entire project and you had to hand it in on time, and it had to be accepted in order to go ahead to the second year.

Most people don't know that dentures are made of acrylic, which is a type of plastic, but first they are made of wax. Then you put the wax denture into what's called a metal flask, pour plaster or stone around it, melt out the wax and replace it with acrylic. That's a very simple explanation of a very difficult process.

About three days before it was due to be handed in I was ready to melt out the wax and replace it with acrylic. It's called "processing the denture."

I had no one to help me, but there was a very kind senior student named Harry, who took pity on me and let me into one of the fraternity houses where the students did their laboratory work. I wasn't a member of any of the fraternities and so theoretically was not allowed in there to do any work.

He had me come in late at night when no one was there and he guided me through this difficult process. If not for him I would have had nowhere to do this.

Talk about fear. The wax has to stay in the boiling water for quite a long time to make sure it's all melted out before you replace it with the acrylic. We waited for what seemed like hours, mixed the acrylic, and placed it where the wax had been, put it back in the boiling water, and waited for more hours until it was processed.

We basically stayed up all night and he stayed with me. And when we opened the flasks to my horror the dentures were ruined. Completely ruined.

The acrylic had something called porosity, which meant there were little holes all over it. Somehow air had gotten incorporated into the acrylic and caused these little holes to form.

I saw my life flash before my eyes. My life was over. If you failed the denture part of the year you failed out of school. I was in such a panic I didn't know what to do.

Harry told me about another senior dental student who he was pretty sure knew how to help me but it was about 4 or 5 A.M., so I had to wait until the next day to see him.

I remember going to his house and ringing his bell and telling him of my plight and that Harry said he'd probably be able to help me. He told me to cover my ruined dentures with wax and do the entire processing over again. It was called "jumping the case."

I don't remember if he came with me or not or if Harry did it with me, but I literally stayed up the entire night again to get it done. Cruelly enough at the very same time that this was going on, I had a gross anatomy exam on the head and brain, which is the most difficult part of the body to be tested on.

As bizarre as it sounds, I had to tell the Gross Anatomy professor that I had no group to work with and he let me sneak a human head out of the lab and take it home in a bag so I could study on my own.

Here I am walking through the streets of Philadelphia at 4 or 5 in the morning in a very bad and dangerous neighborhood with a human head in a bag.

I dissected that head on one end of the only table I had in my apartment and ate on the other end. It was a very sick existence. To this day I don't know how I got it done but somehow I got the dentures finished and passed the Gross Anatomy exam, and believe me it was gross! (LOL) I'm sure that the stress of that experience alone changed me in some way.

In my third year of school I was banned from working in the clinic for three weeks. I was told I was not allowed to see patients until I cut my hair and shaved off my moustache.

Losing three weeks of work almost meant you couldn't get enough done to graduate, and there was no such thing as taking any course over in dental school. If you were out you were out.

During those three weeks my father drove down from New York to see the instructors and try to reason with them. They told him to tell me to get a haircut.

To his credit he told them that he couldn't tell me how to look, and that I was a grown man, and had my own ideas of how I wanted to look, and he had to respect that.

My Dad needed some dental work and they wouldn't even let me in the clinic to work on him, even after all the money he was paying for me to go to school. They softened a bit when they found out he had been in the O.S.S. during World War 2.

I'm surprised they were even impressed with that since it seemed they'd be rooting for the other side.

I remember the Pennsylvania Dutch guy's words exactly. He said, "Your Dad served us well in World War 2." That was very meaningful for him eventually allowing me back in the clinic, because my Dad had served us well in World War 2. First I had to get a wig. Seriously!

No one in my family had ever become a doctor before. I was the first to graduate college and go on from there, and my parents were very proud of me, but they told me many times after getting tearful calls from me that they would support my decision if I wanted to drop out.

I told them I would NEVER let these people get the best of me no matter what I had to do. My mother worked at J.C. Penney and she found a wig for me that had short hair with a part.

She sent it to me by mail, and I went to a local barbershop and had it shaped and fit to my head. I wore it to school and told the Confederate flag guy that I had gotten a haircut the way he wanted. He called me to his office and had me spin slowly in a circle for him to look at me from every angle.

He had no idea it was a wig and okayed me to go back into his clinic if I agreed to keep my hair short like this and keep my moustache curled above my lip which I had to do with moustache wax.

So I went to school looking like a young Salvador Dali with a wig and the ends of my moustache sticking up in the air. I looked like a maniac, but as long as I wore a tie I was okay by them.

I didn't have a date the whole time I was there because I thought to myself, any girl that would be attracted to me the way I had to look was someone I wouldn't want to know.

To show you how disingenuous they were after about a month or so of me wearing the wig, which by the way I wore for the next two years until I graduated, those same two guys told me my hair was growing again and that I should get it cut. They had no idea it was a wig. They just wanted to torture me.

I had an older doctor who was supposedly my advisor who took me out in the hall one day and told me that I was "a disgrace to the profession" and that I would never be successful.

He actually said that because I had a moustache. A disgrace to the profession. That's really great advice and encouragement for a young person to hear.

Meanwhile the halls were filled with paintings of the founders of the school all of whom had mutton chop sideburns, beards and moustaches. The irony was lost on them.

One of the worst examples of how I was treated was when we were learning to give injections in the mouth. I can feel you cringing as you read this. We had lectures on it, but the truth is the only way you can learn to give injections is by actually doing it.

So I was sitting in the clinic with a needle already in the patients gum when an instructor came by, looked at what I was doing and said "Put it in further" then hit my elbow pushing the needle in even further.

I was so horrified I didn't know what to do. Fortunately the patient wasn't hurt. Today that would be considered assault. He should have been arrested.

Until the day I graduated I was mistreated and abused and on the day of graduation as they handed me my diploma one of these jerks said to me, "Gurian get a haircut!" Despite all the abuse I wound up graduating in the top half of my class, number 54 out of 126 students.

Very recently in an interesting turn of events, I was contacted by the current Dean of the dental school from which I graduated who said he wanted to meet with me in New York.

I experienced fear when I got the invitation, because I didn't know what it was about. I asked his secretary if this was going to be a group meeting, and she said, "No, just the two of you." I didn't ask her why he wanted to meet with me because I was nervous to find out.

I agonized over whether to accept the invite, finally deciding that I would attend and tell him my story of how I was treated. I looked at it as an interesting opportunity to finally tell someone what had happened to me. It turned out that he showed up with another Dean as well.

I thought they were going to ask me for a donation because from the day I graduated I never had anything to do with that school. I harbored tremendous resentments against them, and had to work very hard to not believe them telling me that I would never be successful.

They had literally tried to destroy me as a person and especially as a doctor. They tried to take away all of my self-esteem and confidence and told me that I would never succeed or never have any patients. When I graduated I was filled with fear.

I remember having no confidence as I searched for my first job out of school. I got a job in a Medicaid office and wound up running the office for two and a half years. It had four or five chairs and I ran them all. I loved working in that terrible neighborhood and I treated the poor people like they were gold.

They had never had a doctor who treated them that way before and I stayed there for 2 ½ years until I bought my own practice. It took me years to build up my confidence and self-esteem to where I could be successful and let go of all the negativity I was subjected to. It just so happened that I was a very good dentist and really enjoyed the work.

Back to the present, I accepted the meeting with the two Deans with great trepidation, as I didn't know how they would respond to what I planned to tell them. I came to the brunch prepared to tell them my story of how poorly I was treated.

As soon as I started and mentioned the names of the two men who were the worst to me, the main Dean stopped me and said, "They were racists and anti-Semites, and they ruined the reputation of the school."

I was so relieved, and I thanked him sincerely for saying that before I alluded to it, because I had always thought that was what was behind me being treated like that. There were other Jewish students but for some reason I was the one who was singled out and treated the worst.

Not only didn't these Deans want anything from me but they invited me to come down to Philly to the new school as their guests to tell my story to the students. We ended the meeting by taking photos together and exchanging hugs.

It was an amazing feeling of closure for me after all these years. But also a great example of how I show up and confront fear on a continuing basis.

As an interesting update, because of the Covid 19 pandemic, I was not able to go to Philadelphia to lecture to the students, but just today as I am writing this page I have been invited by the Dean to address the alumni and the students on July 15, 2020 in a Zoom presentation about my life, combining dentistry with comedy and how I used positive thinking to help recover from Covid double pneumonia.

And that's what can happen when you confront fear! To me that's amazing.

CHAPTER

3

The Nightmare Of Comedy

MY FEAR OF PERFORMING

If your dream is to perform comedy, the best time to start is in your teens or early 20's when nobody knows you. It gives you the freedom to "bomb" which most new comics do, and which then gives you the freedom to learn from that terrible experience and get better.

No one except you cares if you bomb because nobody knows you. By the time I wanted to start performing I had already worked with too many famous people and the industry knew who I was even if the public didn't. It felt like too much pressure and it kept me off the stage for many years.

This was one of the biggest fears I ever had to face, and I feel anxiety to this day when I go on stage. But when I interviewed Jim Gaffigan he told me that he got physically ill for about the first six years of his career, every time he had to go on stage, which made me feel a little better. I didn't get sick. I just didn't do it.

This is my story of how I got involved in comedy and finally wound up on stage.

From the time I was only 12 years old I had a love for comedy and was already writing and creating things for the amusement of my friends.

At the tender age of 12 I had already decided to be a dentist and was already writing comedy!

I wrote absurd stories and made up ridiculous names, and got other kids to say them, which made me laugh more than them. I taught older kids bizarre dances and words I made up, and for some strange reason they did the dances and said the words.

Even as a young child, whenever there was a comedian on TV I would run into the room to watch. I attribute this early love for comedy to my Dad, Raymond Gurian who had a great sense of humor himself and loved to make up silly words. He was always cracking jokes and had a kind word for everyone.

I was always in trouble in school for making the other kids laugh. That seemed to be my raison d'etre for attending class. I was a nuisance but the teachers put up with it. One teacher wrote in my yearbook. "What would I have done without your impish face popping up in front of me all year?"

In junior high school I stole the math teacher's roll book so he couldn't take attendance, and assigned each row a different noise to make upon my signal just to disrupt the class.

One row would tap their feet, another row would tap their pencils on the desk, and a third row would clear their throats or cough. Again why they listened to me I'll never really know but they did.

In junior high in art class we had a teacher named Mrs. Goldstein who would check that we had our art supplies every session. She would say "Row 1 hold up your ruler." And each kid would have to hold up their ruler, and they did, ... except for me. And she would say "Gurian where's your ruler?" And I had the nerve to tell her that it was stuck in my desk and I couldn't get it out.

I even made believe I was trying to pull it out. She would start to walk over to help me but before she got there I "managed" to pull it out to show her.

Then she'd say, "Row 1 hold up your crayons!" And every kid would do it except for me. I can't believe I had the utter gall to do this with everything she asked us to hold up. According to me, each item was always stuck in my desk. How I had the nerve to keep doing that I'll never understand, but I did.

I used to like to shoot spitballs through a straw, so another time I brought a straw to class and complained to her that someone was shooting spit balls at me. It was actually me doing it to other kids, but I told her that someone was shooting spit balls and hitting me in the neck.

She became incensed and lectured the class that you could take someone's eye out with a spit ball. I probably should explain that spit balls were just tiny pieces of wet paper, often wet with saliva that you could shoot through a straw, and hit other kids if you had good aim.

I happened to have great aim. I actually flipped one with my fingernail at the kid behind me and it flew directly up his nose. Right up his nostril and he started to gag and threw up on his desk. I'll never forget it!

Anyway Miss Goldstein made me the monitor and had me stand in the back of the class to watch and see who was shooting the spit balls. My back was against the back wall so there was no way that the following could have happened, but I still insisted that someone was shooting spit balls at me even though it was physically impossible for that to happen.

I would make believe I had to throw something away and walk behind the teacher who was lecturing to the class and do a silly dance behind her to make the other kids laugh.

I also used to take the kid's lunch who sat in front of me and surreptitiously put it under his foot, which was kind of raised up in the air. He sat with his toes on the floor and his heel up in the air so I slipped his sandwich under his foot and at the end of the class he stood up on his lunch.

At the time it was funny to me. Today it sounds mean! (LOL)

My mother had to sign a note about my conduct every day, and I had to show it to my teacher to make sure she saw that my mother had seen it.

I was in the band and played the huge tympani drums. I got thrown out of graduation because I brought in plastic spiders and put them on the drums so that when I hit the drums the plastic spiders flew up in the air onto the girls playing the violin, who would then scream and interrupt the song we were playing.

That got me thrown out of graduation only a few days before the ceremony. I don't remember if they let me back in.

Even in college during chemistry class when the class was very quiet and the teacher was writing on the board, I had the nerve to make a very loud noise as if no one sitting next to me, or around me would know that it was me.

I did it all throughout the term and at the end of the year the teacher said to me, "Do you really think I didn't know it was you making that noise all year long?" And I was like "What noise?"

I taught myself to kind of "step outside myself" to give me the "courage" to do those kinds of things.

My Dad had a great sense of humor and a great love of comedy and used to take me to the movies to see comedy shows with Laurel and Hardy, The Marx Brothers, and Abbott and Costello. What kills me is that they're still funny today but if they came around they probably couldn't even get representation.

Somewhere along the way I developed a love for W.C. Fields, and produced W.C. Fields nights in my college, along with a couple of hootenannies, which is a word you'll have to Google.

I went through a period of time when I actually thought I was the re-incarnation of W.C. Fields because he was all I could think about. I was obsessed and used to talk like him when speaking to girls. "Hello my little dear! My tiny hen!"

When I was 16 years old my girlfriend at the time made me something that I have to this day. It was a spider that looked like W.C. Fields with a big red nose and a top hat.

I had forgotten to mention that I was fascinated by spiders even though I was simultaneously afraid and disgusted by them and so began my history of spider-walking.

This was not easy for me to do by any means, and would set the stage for me to become less self-conscious in order to do acting and perform on stage in the future. I would challenge myself to do things that would make me feel uncomfortable or embarrassed.

It's very common to see teenage boys doing silly things for the amusement of their friends. That's too easy. One day I thought to myself, what if I could get myself to do those kinds of things when I was all alone. That would be the height of freedom if I was able to do that. No audience, just do it for my own amusement.

So I got up the nerve to try walking through the streets of The Bronx like a spider, or what I thought a spider would look like if it was walking through the streets, and again I would challenge myself by doing this when I was alone, so people would not think I was doing it for the amusement of my friends.

For some reason this was important to me, so that I knew that I was doing this all for myself and not to make my friends laugh. The danger is that people who see you doing these kinds of things all by yourself will think that you're insane.

Well this kind of backfired on me because unbeknownst to me, my mother's sister, my dear Aunt Joan, saw me in the street walking very low, with my hands behind my back, stopping every so often to play a little flute I had in my pocket. I came home that day to find her in tears telling my mother that she was afraid they'd have to put me in an institution because I was walking in the street all alone in a very unusual manner!

It took me a while to convince her that I was really ok and was just doing it as kind of an experiment.

I also used to do it while I was driving. I once got stopped by a cop for walking like a spider in traffic with a friend of mine who I also encouraged to do the same thing.

I was driving my Dad's car. We had stopped for a red light on the Grand Concourse which was a major thoroughfare in The Bronx, and we both got out of the car and walked low around the other cars that were stopped around us.

Before we could get back in the car I heard yelling and it was a cop who grabbed us both and demanded to know what we were doing.

I remember standing on the curb with my friend Dave, the both of us wearing love beads, and the only thing I could come up with for a reason why we were walking like that in traffic was, "Sorry officer, we haven't seen each other for a long time!"

And HE said, "Is that a reason to do something so dangerous? Don't you realize that the other people in their cars don't know what you're doing, and in some cases can't even see you?"

All I could think of was I hope my parents don't find out, and after a while he finally let us go with a stern warning, and no ticket. There probably was no ticketable offense in the books yet for walking like a spider, ... in traffic no less.

Many years later, I used traffic again in making my short film "Men Who Dance In Traffic With the Sunday Edition of the New York Times." It was part of my "Men Who" Series, a series of short films about men who do very unusual things. It came out of my meeting with Woody Allen.

Around the time I was in dental school I decided that there were only three people or entities in the world that I needed to meet, Woody Allen, Salvador Dali, and The Beach Boys. All were very important to me at that time and before.

The Beach Boys music had gotten me through the depression of high school, which is a difficult time for just about everyone. It's why I can never understand people who insist that high school was the best time of their lives.

Salvador Dali represented to me the height of absurdism, which I took into my comedy. I considered what I did as surrealistic comedy, (more on that later!) And Woody Allen was my idol comedically.

In those days we bought comedy albums and played them over and over again. I'd go over to my friend Dave's house and we'd listen to Woody's stories, one in particular about him going hunting, and shooting a moose.

Turns out that the moose was only knocked unconscious and "came to" while tied to his fender driving home.

Not knowing what to do he decided to take the live moose to a costume party, and passed it off as a Jewish couple named The Solomons, supposedly a married couple dressed as a moose.

In Woody's story, at the end of the evening they have a "Best Costume" contest where the best costume of the evening award goes to the Berkowitz's, a married couple dressed as a moose. The real moose comes in second, is furious and locks horns with the Berkowitz's.

It was that kind of humor that inspired me, plus a story he performed on The Ed Sullivan Show where he was walking down the street when a maniac threw a Bible out of the window and hit him in the chest, and had he not just happened to have had a bullet in his breast pocket that deflected the Bible, the Bible would have pierced his heart. I loved that kind of humor.

At the time I was doing little films and writing bizarre stories like "Several men were arrested for smearing cream cheese on the ankles of elderly women who wore their stockings rolled down like bagels."

If you've ever seen the old women with the stockings rolled down around their ankles it always looked like bagels to me, so I got my dear grandmother, Nana Fay to let me put cream cheese on her ankles.

She made believe she had a heavy Jewish accent and told her story to the camera. Her name in the sketch was Mrs. O'Goyim who had recently come over from Ireland. She agreed to the interview on the stipulation that she remain anonymous, so I put a Groucho Marx nose and moustache on her and only referred to her as Mrs. X.

Concerning the cream cheese, she explained, “You know in the Jewish religion we have two kinds of stockings, one for milk and one for meat, and this crazy man schmeared cream cheese all over my meat stockings and I can’t get it off!” And my super 8 camera zoomed in on her ankles with the cream cheese.

This was one of the films I brought up to Saturday Night Live in 1977 and showed to now award winning writer/producer/director Alan Zweibel who I still speak to and who remembers that film to this day.

He started me on my comedy writing career, by calling his manager at the time, a man named David Jonas, who was managing the late Freddie Prinze and had gotten him the sit-com Chico and The Man.

What was particularly special was that Alan didn’t just give me David’s number, he personally called him on my behalf. That was a special thing to do!

But I digress! I did a “special” on “Prominent Businessmen Who Wear Swimfins To The Office” and in one of the scenes, I snuck into a real hospital at night with a real surgeon and a surgical crew to film a heart surgeon who supposedly wears swim-fins in the operating room during heart surgery, to prove that it was true.

I also filmed a famous jingle writer in his studio, who claimed that wearing swimfins gave him the creativity he needed to do his work, a famous psychologist who claimed that his patients felt more comfortable when he was wearing swim fins, and a successful accountant who claimed that not only was he the first black accountant to wear swimfins to the office he was also the first white accountant to wear swimfins to the office.

And I created "The Masters of Disguise" which started out as two master criminals who disguised themselves as inanimate objects to commit their crimes.

It started with two men disguised as coats who robbed a hat store, Nat Snatz's Hats. They came in folded over the arms of two other men, and said "Just act natural like we're your coats and nobody'll get hurt."

Police artists drew composite drawings of the perpetrators and of course it was two coats. One man was described as looking like a tan trench coat with epaulets and a belt, the other was described as resembling an overcoat, possibly black but maybe navy blue.

In a similar crime by the Masters of Disguise, two men disguised as a pair of eyeglasses robbed a local optometrist shop by coming in on another man's face. I always did interviews with the "victims", and this man said, "I don't know what's going on. I was walking into this eyeglass place to get my glasses adjusted when all of a sudden, out of nowhere another pair of glasses jumps onto my face and a voice says "Just act natural like we're your glasses and no one will get hurt. What's this city coming to?"

This eventually escalated to 250,000 men disguised as vests who rob a suit warehouse of a quarter of a million suits, and I interview the designer who tells me, "I only design two piece suits. I went to my warehouse today and all 250,000 suits had vests. I didn't know what to do. I went out to lunch and when I came back all the suits were gone. It had to be the vests!"

Needless to say police artists threatened to strike rather than have to try and draw all 250,000 vests, and it was a very dramatic moment!

So while I was in dental school I decided that it was imperative that I meet Woody Allen. On the rare occasions when I could come home to New York for a weekend I would go to the theatre on Broadway where Woody was starring in a play called "Play It Again Sam" with Tony Roberts who was in many of Woody's projects in those days.

I would drop off little notes written on the back of my dental school cards that I gave to patients in the clinic who had appointments. I would write things as if I knew Woody, ... things like, "Hi Woody I haven't seen you in so long. I'll be coming to the show soon, and I'll bring my cardboard thumb."

I thought it was necessary to inject some bizarre statement like that to catch his attention. I kept this up for several months as I recall, always dropping off notes on my little appointment cards.

Finally I saved up enough money for tickets to the show, which was probably the last time I ever paid for a show, and I made my plan.

I had never met such a big star before and I knew it was important that you come across as a sane person, realizing that most men have no interest in meeting strangers, in the form of young men after their show.

I came to the conclusion that in order to appear sane you either had to wear a tie, or bring a pretty girl with you, which was not the first of my unusual and mostly incorrect thoughts.

I didn't have a tie and I only knew one pretty girl and she hated me. Her name was Leslie. We had recently broken up and she really wanted nothing to do with me. However she knew that meeting Woody Allen was my dream so I begged her to accompany me, and she accepted.

The night of the show I dropped off my last card with the stage manager and it said, "Woody I'm here and I'll be back to see you during intermission." I didn't know that it's more proper to wait until the end of the show and not bother someone during the intermission. But there were lots of things I didn't know then. I was only around 23 years old.

Intermission comes and I get nervous. Really nervous, ... and I'm almost ready to chicken out, but Leslie insists that I go because she came with me.

We go out to the street and open the stage door and the stage manager is not in his seat. There's no one there so I take her hand and run up the stairs, but the stairs led to the roof.

We come back down and the stage manager is there now and he says to me, "Can I help you?" And

I say, "Yes, Woody's expecting me." And he says, "Well then go right in."

It was that easy in those days. Pre-terrorism. It was a much more relaxed world. So we go to Woody's dressing room and it's empty. He's down the hall in Tony Robert's dressing room with the entire cast.

I remember this like it was yesterday. Now I'm really nervous.

Once again I try to back out but Leslie is insistent that I don't. I walk up to the room with great trepidation. I look in and Woody is sitting on a couch facing the door where I'm standing. I look at him, and crook my finger calling him over like you would do to a child.

He looks at me and silently mouths the word "Me?" And I shake my head yes. He walks over and he's actually holding my card, and he says to me, "You must be Jeff", and at that moment meeting my idol I get so excited that I start saying very bizarre things to him like "Let's open up a day camp and throw winter clothes at people", and "Let's walk low like we used to in Europe!"

And he looks at Leslie and says, "This guy's a f*@kin' nut!" and I realize I have to calm down. So I tell him I'm a comedy writer and that I write things that people say were very Woody Allen-ish and that I was hoping I could show him my writing.

To which he says, "Well, I'm in the middle of a show right now. Do you think you could come back tomorrow night?" To which I immediately respond, "No, I'm sorry I'm much too busy."

I actually said, "Yes, of course I'll come back tomorrow night." But he says, "Not during intermission. At the end of the show."

So the next night I beg Leslie to come back with me because I didn't have the self-esteem to show up on my own. That came back to haunt me many years later when I did something similar and ruined my opportunity to make short films for Saturday Night Live. Suffice it to say that I had so little confidence in myself, I was sure I needed someone special on my arm to be validated. I didn't realize that it was me and only me who had gotten me this far.

Next night comes and it's a horrible rainstorm. I get Leslie from Co-Op City, in my father's car, and we drive down to meet Woody. But this time I'm much more relaxed and I say to him, "You know, the Aztecs weren't too good at tap dancing but boy could they sway!"

I was very into the concept of swaying in those days, kind of like what people did in the 1940's when they heard the national anthem. In all the old newsreels it seemed that people would start swaying any time they had the opportunity. No one sways anymore!

After the show he takes me into a little dressing room where we sit and he reads all of my material.

As I recall it wasn't even written out in script form. It was little scraps of paper in an envelope with concepts written on them. He reads through every one.

My dream was that he'd say to me, "As soon as I'm done with this play we must go on the road together and make movies."

Surprisingly enough he doesn't say that. What he does say is that my material is very visual and that I should think of making a film out of it, which I did some years later.

First I had to graduate from Dental School and get set up in my life. But years later when I became friends with Jack Rollins who managed Woody for his entire career, until Jack passed away in 2015 at 100 years old, he told me that Woody must have really seen something special in me for him to have invited me back like that.

He said it wasn't his nature to do that!

Jack went on to be very helpful to me in my career and sent me up to SNL to meet with Herb Sargent the long time main comedy writer on the show for so many years.

When I met Herb and asked him if he read any of my material he said, "I don't even have to. If Jack Rollins says you're funny, you're funny!"

Some years later I took those early ideas that I showed Woody and actually did make films out of them. They were short films called "The Men Who Series" about men who did very unusual things.

They played at Carolines Comedy Club as part of the Toyota Comedy Festival and they had names like "Men Who Take A Pitchfork To The Movies", "Men Who Enjoy Latin Dancing With Tools", and "Men Who Dance Where They're Not Supposed To", starring none other than Peter Dinklage, who went on to become one of the biggest stars in the world after starring in the HBO hit "Game of Thrones."

I just realized that none of this backstory had to do with performing comedy but it gives you some background as to how I even got into the comedy field.

In 1980 I got to write for one of the biggest comedy stars in the world, Rodney Dangerfield. Rodney used to do my material on The Tonight

Show with Johnny Carson, and in his act at his club and on the road. I couldn't have been more excited.

I went on to write for and befriend many of the big stars of the day in what is known as "The Golden Age of Comedy." Milton Berle became my sponsor in The Friars Club, and I got to work with him, and Jerry Lewis, Henny Youngman, Red Buttons, Allen and Rossi, Sid Caesar, Rich Little, Joey Adams, Dick Shawn, Myron Cohen, Joan Rivers and more.

With Milton Berle at the L.A. Friars Club in 1985

I also got to work with newcomers in those days like Richard Belzer, Gilbert Gottfried, Phil Hartman and Kevin Nealon from SNL, George Wallace and even Andrew "Dice" Clay.

Very few people can say they had the honor of writing for "Dice." He's talked about it on Sirius XM and recently backstage at a comedy club called "The Stand" in NYC, he had me tell his people the story of how we met.

Besides his bodyguard and the owner of the club, I was the only one he let come backstage to hang out with him.

With "Dice" backstage at The Stand
Comedy Club in NYC-9/27/19

So the point of all this is that I was not performing for most of those years. I was just writing and trying to make a name for myself. During that time, people in the business encouraged me to do stand-up but I was too nervous.

As I stated earlier, if you start performing in your 20's when no one knows you, you have the freedom to bomb and be horrible, and no one will care because they expect that from you. And that's how you get better.

You keep going up on stage until you get the hang of being comfortable and knowing what's funny. But again, by the time I was ready to start performing I faced a lot of fear because too many people already knew of me. I was what you might call an "industry name." The public hadn't heard of me but people in the business did, and it felt like a lot of pressure to be funny right away.

It wasn't until about 15 years ago or so that I got the courage to get up and perform at a place called Surf Reality down on the Lower East Side of NYC, run by a guy named Rob Pritchard.

As I recall he had a show every Sunday night MC'ed by a guy named Faceboy. He called himself Faceboy because he was totally bald so his face never ended. It went all the way up to the top of his head.

They had a lottery show where you would put your name in a hat when you arrived and they would pick the names and that's the order you would perform in.

Everyone would get a chance even if it took until 2 or 3 in the morning.

I was going for a while just to watch and some of the people were so horrible, I realized I couldn't be worse. I had to just step outside of myself, detach from fear, like I did when I got myself to spider-walk, and get up there on stage and try it out.

I figured the worst I could do would be to embarrass myself, and embarrassment is just a thought that I create, ... and any thought I create I can also un-create!

The first time I thought I might faint, but I did it for a while, week after week, and from what I recall it went pretty well. My next memory is doing it at a place called Club 13, which was a mistake because it was sandwiched in between musical acts.

Then I took a performance class with a guy named Steve Rosenfield and that was great, and for graduation I got to perform at Stand Up New

York and Carolines Comedy Club. We got to do two shows to a packed room and it was very exciting.

After that I recall getting up one night at the old New York Comedy Club and Artie Lange's sidekick Mike Bochetti happened to be there, and told me I was great and really encouraged me.

Since then I've been performing on the regular at every club in NY except the Comedy Cellar, and I've been on the stage of most of the big clubs in LA.

Stand up comedy is one of the hardest things to do. To stand up on a stage all alone and try to convince strangers that what you think is funny is actually funny is a very daunting task. But I do it every chance I get!

Killing it on stage at the legendary Comic Strip!

CHAPTER

4

Confronting Uncomfortability

MY SOLO TRIP TO EUROPE

Once again I'm going to repeat that everything makes me uncomfortable. Well, ... almost everything. And why I repeat, is because as I said earlier, no one learns anything by hearing it once.

The first time you hear something maybe it makes sense to you, and you learn it "intellectually", but you don't truly learn it until you take it into your heart, and that trip is a different length for each person. You have to really internalize something before you can say you learned it, and that takes lots of repetition.

No one goes to the gym once and leaves with the body they want, and nobody takes one piano lesson and winds up performing in Carnegie Hall.

Every athlete knows that you must work out every day in order to excel in whatever you choose to do.

So I try and make myself do things that make me uncomfortable, that the rest of the world seems to do much more easily.

Take traveling for instance. Traveling is very hard for me. My ADHD is severe and causes me a lot of confusion. And it's my understanding that each person with ADHD has different symptoms. One of mine is a complete lack of direction.

If I go someplace and had to make a right turn to get there, intellectually I know I have to make a left turn to get back, but when I get to the place where I have to make that turn I can't see it.

I can literally go someplace for years and one day it won't look familiar to me at all. This causes me great confusion and makes traveling very difficult because I'm always lost and have to depend on strangers to help me out.

To give you some idea of how bad I am, I always thought that North was the way you were facing. I didn't know it was always in the same place. I thought it was relative. If you're going in this direction then that's North. The one thing I was sure of is that South was always behind me!

For me, the invention of the GPS was a godsend. The most amazing invention ever. Before that I had to ask people to kindly write down directions for me when I drove, saying things like "Go three blocks and make a right then another two blocks and make a left" and I had to hold those papers on the steering wheel as I drove, referring to them constantly, which was not particularly the safest or most comfortable way to travel.

In my quest to challenge myself to travel I went to Europe alone twice and recently went to Japan all by myself. That trip itself will be covered in a later chapter. Talk about a challenge! I may never fully recover!(LOL)

Some people go to Europe when they're still in their teens, ... that is unless you are actually from Europe. Then there's a good chance you not only went much earlier, you were probably even born there. This chapter may not be for you! (LOL)

But for United States citizens, going to Europe is supposedly a way of growing up. A way of expanding your mind, and exhibiting your maturity. It's almost a "right of passage."

These days, it's not unusual for teenagers to go "abroad", as they say, as a high school graduation present. College students often get a chance to go as foreign exchange students.

I didn't do any of that. Growing up in The Bronx when I did, it was a big thing to take the bus to Fordham Road, which was a big shopping area at the time, about a twenty minute ride from where I lived.

No one went to Europe in those days. At least no one I knew. I had a very middle class upbringing. If you went up to the Catskill Mountains during the summer, and stayed in a bungalow colony, you were considered a traveler.

Traveling to Europe never really interested me. That was for someone else. I like New York. Why would I want to go to other countries that have less than I have right here in New York? I could never come up with a satisfactory answer to that one, so I never went.

Until 2008. For some reason, it suddenly dawned on me that life was moving on, and like it or not, I was getting older, and if I was ever going to go to Europe, it would be important to go while I could still walk well. Plus, there were probably things there that might be nice to see.

Now don't get me wrong. It's not like I never went anywhere. I had been to Mexico, Hawaii, San

Juan, St. Thomas, St, Lucia, Toronto, Montreal, California, and a few other places in the States.

But the way I thought about it was like this: Hawaii was probably the most beautiful place I ever went. So what? What good does that do me today? I saw it. I enjoyed it. But what good did it do me? Was my life any better or more advanced for me having experienced that?

If I go away for two weeks, my work piles up, my mail piles up, my bills pile up, my e-mails certainly pile up, and for what? So I could see things I've always read about like The Colosseum, the Via Veneto, the Costa Del Sol, or The Sistine Chapel?

Is that really important to me? It wasn't up until then. But my ADHD causes confusion, and not only fears of getting lost, but also fears of losing things.

Usually the thing you need the most like your passport, or your credit card, or your cell phone. It seems to be very tied in with self-sabotage, something I consider myself an expert about, and will address later on in this book!

It also makes you fearful of not being able to be organized enough to travel from city to city, and make your connections, without something terrible happening.

Because I believe in confronting my fears, which is the only way to make them disappear, I decided that this year, in 2008, I was going to use my two weeks vacation time to go to Europe. Great! Now where in Europe was I going to go?

When I travel, things happen to me that happen to no one else. I know, because I look around. Never have I seen another person with the material of his sport jacket literally caught in the zipper of his luggage, which happened to me, requiring me to run across the airport attached to my suitcase to try and make my flight.

I looked like a spider, which might have been karma for all those times I tried walking like one, or like Groucho Marx when he used to walk very low in his old movies.

Never have I seen another person whose luggage cart tips over incessantly, while he's dragging huge, heavy bags through the airport running to catch his plane, because he mistook his aisle number for the gate number of where the plane was leaving from.

Invariably my life turns into a Woody Allen movie, and I can't seem to do anything about it.

As a hint of what's to come on this trip, I got locked in a bathroom in Barcelona, lost my luggage in Malaga, fell asleep on a bus in Marbella, got left off three miles from my destination on a strange highway, and my passport and traveler's checks were found laying in the gutter in Rome.

Thank G-d some honest person in Italy called out to me to try and get my attention, but I was trying my best to ignore the man, because I thought he was just making rude noises at me.

That has happened to me before, but more-so in the United States, so in general I just try and ignore people on the street who try and get my attention.

Finally I turned around and saw that he was really just trying to return my passport and traveler's checks, which had fallen out of my fanny pack and into the street. And on and on!

Anyway, Europe itself is not just one country. It's many countries, none of which I had ever visited, so how do you choose your itinerary?

Friends of mine told me politely that I wasn't cut out for the kind of tours where everything is planned out for you, and where you travel in the same group every day for the whole trip.

Most of the time you start out as early as 7:30 in the morning, and go from city to city until you drop from exhaustion, reminding me of that 70's flick, "If It's Tuesday, This Must Be Belgium."

They suggested I make my own tour. Being that I speak fairly good Spanish, or so I thought until I tried to use it, I chose Spain as one of my destinations. Now do I go to Madrid, Seville, Barcelona, the Costa Del Sol? So many choices.

Most travel agents combine a trip to Spain with a trip to Portugal, so I thought that was the way to go, until I realized that I should go where I wanted to go. It was my itinerary to create, so I should just choose where I wanted to go.

Nothing against Portugal, but I've always been interested in the ancient world, particularly ancient Rome, so Italy seemed to be the next best choice in that regard. Okay, Spain and Italy it is.

I always liked the beach, and have always heard of places like Mallorca, Malaga, and Ibiza, (pronouncing the "z" like a "th", as people did who went there and wanted to sound sophisticated!)! I thought that would make a good place to start.

I chose Marbella, a place I had been hearing about forever. It sounded exotic and brought to mind extremely tan, gorgeous girls, yachts, and the potential for fabulous parties. I thought I'd start there for three days, and then move on to

Barcelona, another city known for it's beauty, and stay there three days as well.

Then I would fly to Italy to visit Rome and Florence. Originally I thought I'd go to Rome first, and then Florence, but because you can not fly home to the United States directly from Florence, the day I was leaving, I would have to take a train from Florence to Rome, and then a cab to the airport. Too much tension.

So I decided that I'd land in Rome, and take a train to Florence for three days. Then take the train back to Rome, and stay for four more days, then go right to the airport and fly back to The States.

That was my plan. Stay tuned!

THE PLAN

I found a travel agent through a recommendation, and he was nice enough, ... as long as I called him at the right time. The first time I called, I left a message. He called me back, and left his cell phone number. I called him back around 8 P.M. thinking that if he left me his cell number, he wanted me to call him when I could.

When he answered, he seemed surprised that I called, and gently reminded me that I was calling after hours, and that his cell number should be used only during working hours. I didn't see the point, but I didn't want to argue with a man I hadn't met yet.

Our next conversation was not much more comfortable. He kept mentioning how busy he was, until I finally said, "Look, if you're too busy to handle my business, I'll call someone else." That seemed to change his tone, and we got down to the business of building my itinerary.

He wavered from being helpful with making suggestions, concerning modes of travel, and hotels, to expecting me to read the ton of literature he gave me about each country and possible tours that were offered, and to make my own decisions.

We spent time in his office, where he took me on a tour of the very large premises, and we huddled at his desk until we chose the itinerary, after which he acted as if he didn't want me to drop by again. Instead he said he preferred e-mail for any questions. A very strange man to say the least!

Delta was one of the only carriers to fly directly, and that was the plan, so we decided to use them. I would fly Delta to Madrid, wait three hours for an Iberia flight to Malaga, and then make my way somehow to Marbella. That was the first part of my trip, and the main thing I focused on, because with ADHD if I focus on too many details, I get very confused, and overwhelmed. That's when the fear takes over.

Leaving Marbella I would fly Spanair to Barcelona, where I'd make my way to the Hotel Regina. Then Air Italia would take me to Rome where I would catch the Euro-Rail to Florence, which you should learn to refer to as Firenze, because if you look for signs to Florence, you'll be standing in the train station for months!

In Florence I'd stay at the Hotel Brunelleschi, and then I'd take the Euro-Rail back to Rome for four days and stay at the Hotel Beverly Hills, which sounded much more like where I was used to going, but was actually nothing like Beverly Hills. Very nice, but nothing like Beverly Hills.

Because of my ADHD I began packing about seven days before I was scheduled to leave. I have learned that I must start packing several days in advance in order to curb the fear of forgetting something important.

Part of my preparation is that I also choose the outfit I'm going to wear to travel several days before, so that I can pack my pockets in advance with certain things that I could not allow myself to forget.

I imagine there are people who show up at the airport and realize they forgot to bring their passport, but I wouldn't know how to handle that without going insane, so I place mine in the inside pocket of the jacket I plan to wear, several days before I leave.

I also place my airline tickets in there, unless they're e-tickets. Then I print out several copies of the confirmation, and my entire itinerary and put one in my pocket, and the rest throughout my luggage.

I also am not able to shop off the rack, so I must select in advance any clothing I could not afford to lose, should my bags get misplaced, because we've all heard the horror stories of people left on vacation with absolutely no clothing. Another thing I couldn't survive.

So I have to try and picture in my mind what clothing is irreplaceable, pack that in a carry-on bag, plus a few days worth of underwear, socks, and personal items, and to plan that all out ahead of time made that even harder, and more of a challenge.

Since 9/11 we're not allowed to bring any liquids on the plane over 2 ounces, so it meant I couldn't pack my cosmetics until the morning of the flight, until I saw what I needed to use to get ready to travel, and then I had to pack the rest to take with me.

I also spent the night before I left, lying stiffly on an old set of sheets, so as not to ruin my good sheets with the residue from the spray-on tan I got to look "healthy" when I got to Marbella. I didn't want to show up on an exotic beach looking like the palest man on the planet.

I had let my best friend talk me into getting one of those spray tans, not realizing that the color would come off on everything that touched my body. To make it worse I had invited my girlfriend to spend that last night with me.

She wound up lying next to me, unable to even touch me, or kiss me goodbye, for fear of smearing this "tan", that I agreed to, so I wouldn't subject myself to the cancer-causing tanning machines I had been so prone to using previously.

Note: Some years later I actually did wind up with skin cancer. Three times I had to have surgery to have the growths removed. Two basal cell carcinomas and one squamous cell. That's because I did things like taking a sun reflector to Puerto Rico! Who does that? (Rhetorical question!) I wound up in the hospital!

Anyway, I awoke in the morning to find I had changed my race. They told me I'd look darker after ten to twelve hours, but I was unrecognizable. Fortunately, they also told me that when I showered, it would mellow out the tan a little bit.

Thank G-d for that, or I might have considered canceling my trip. By the time I scrubbed myself off in the shower, I had an even, normal looking tan. All over!

Europe, here I come! And in deference to my ADHD I took copious daily notes about my trip because otherwise I would totally forget all the details and it would just be a blur.

In the following pages I will share with you in detail the day to day struggle of my travels and you will see why traveling is very difficult for me, and how we, or at least "I" tend to manifest my worst fears.

You'll also see how I confronted every one of mine, including my fears of not being able to meet anyone, which is why I also mention some of the wonderful women I met along the way.

DAY 1

I had a 2:45 car to the airport for a 7:15 P.M. flight. I take no chances on being late. Especially at this time. It was seven years after 9/11 and the anti-terrorist restrictions were still really heavy.

No bombs, serrated knives or long Samurai swords were allowed on the plane anymore, so I took that into consideration when I packed! (LOL)

Actually not even toothpaste was allowed anymore. All liquids were banned from being carried onto the plane.

My car came early. I started videotaping my trip when the doorman rang the bell to tell me the car was here. I had bought one of those folding luggage carts on wheels to help me carry my huge suitcase, my garment bag, and my camera bag, which I needed to hold the digital video camera, a regular video camera, and an old-school 35 mm. camera that used film that I had packed. I wasn't taking any chances on missing anything.

I also had to bring all the instruction booklets for the cameras, because with my ADHD, I can use something a million times, and then suddenly one day, I won't know how to use it at all.

I got to my car to find my driver was a Chinese woman named Lisa, who didn't speak much English. I took that as a good sign, because my girlfriend was also a Chinese woman who did not speak much English.

Lisa grabbed my bags, and threw them into the trunk like they were weightless, and she may not have known English, but she sure knew her directions.

I filmed her along the way. Traffic was insane, and we didn't get to JFK airport until about 4 P.M. I still had 3 hours and 15 minutes to make my flight. As we drove in, I felt sorry for the poor schlubs who were waiting on some crazy long line outside of the terminal.

Moments later, I became one of those "poor schlubs" myself as I joined the end of the line. By 6:45, we were still on line, although I had finally reached the inside of the terminal. I was panicking. Things were moving so slowly that they were taking people off the line so they wouldn't miss their flights.

Fortunately I was able to get someone's attention and told them my flight was at 7:15. They took me off the line, but my flight wound up not taking off until about 8 P.M.

I had requested an exit row, (for more room!), with an aisle seat, and I got what I asked for. I had no seatmate, but because it was an exit row, the divider between the seats didn't lift up, so I couldn't sleep across the seats.

I hadn't had the chance to try out my luggage cart at home, or truthfully even had the thought to do so, so as a lesson to me, on the way to the plane, my luggage cart must have overturned at least three times.

It was not well balanced to say the least, and after the third time of having to put it back together, I was not well balanced either!

In all of my traveling, I saw not one other person whose luggage cart kept tipping over, with his luggage spilling out all over the ground. Not one person! People were looking at me wherever I went. I spent a lot of time on the ground re-organizing my things.

As we were called to board, I'm wheeling my stuff down the corridor that leads to the plane, and as we get to the door of the plane, where you're greeted by the pilot and flight attendants, I have to stop, stoop down, undo the elastic bungee cord holding my luggage, undo the bags, then fold up the cart.

My having to stoop down and undo my bags stops the boarding line, and people behind me are anxious to get on the plane. Even though all that takes maybe a minute or so, it feels like an hour as all eyes stare at me for being the "weirdo" that holds up the line.

Then, with my arms totally full, with the cart and my camera bag both in one hand, and my large, bulging garment bag in the other hand, I have to make my way down an aisle that's too narrow even for skeletally thin people who aren't carrying anything in each hand. Needless to say, I get stuck on almost every seat. Everyone is still staring at me. I'm almost used to it.

I finally find my seat, get my stuff in the overhead bin, and I'm ready to relax.

Seven hours later, we arrived in Madrid. It's 9 A.M. Sitting up front as I was, I was one of the first people off the plane, but because I had to stoop down again and re-assemble my luggage cart, balance my bags on it, and try and secure them with the bungee-type elastic cord, about two hundred people got in front of me.

On my way to the Baggage Claim area, my carry-on luggage turned over again at least twice. They had no escalators to go downstairs where the baggage claim actually was, so each time I got to a staircase, I had to take the luggage off the cart, and carry everything down the stairs by hand. Wonderful! By the time I finally got there, I was on the end of a huge line.

I waited at the carousel almost an hour, but my luggage never came. Everyone else had left, and I was standing there alone. Perfect! Talk about manifesting your worst fears! And to make matters worse, I had to catch my connecting flight.

Fortunately, I speak some Spanish, but it's mostly conversational, not about what to do if you lose your luggage, however I managed to make myself understood. While I'm on line to report my luggage missing, and after trying to explain my situation to several workers, I look at my claim tag and I notice that it lists my flight as going to Malaga.

I asked a woman working there if there's any chance they could have sent my bags to Malaga. She looks at the claim tag and says, "Of course. That's where they are. They sent them to your final destination."

Wouldn't it have been nice if someone at Delta in New York had told me that when I checked my bag in the first place that it was going straight to Malaga? It would have saved me a lot of aggravation.

I started out with three hours to get to my Iberia connecting flight for Malaga. Now I had less than two. Next problem, Iberia was not in this terminal, but in Terminal #4, which was pretty far away, and I had to go upstairs to find the particular bus that would take me there.

THE BUS TO THE TRAIN

I went upstairs, and finally found the right bus to take me to Terminal 4, and now it's 11:30, and I just got to Gate 86 where my flight leaves for Malaga. Thank Goodness I had that three hour layover. I never would have made it if I had any less time.

Security questions my dental instruments, which are sharp, and I'm forced to explain that I used to be a dentist, (true) and that's why I have them. They confer quickly and decide to let me on the plane with them. I guess no planes have ever been hijacked using a dental explorer, sharp and scary looking as it may be!

We land in Malaga. I'm at luggage carousel #27 waiting patiently while everyone else on the plane collects their luggage. Even the young beauty that struck up a conversation with me, finally found her almost missing bag laying next to the conveyor belt, but once again, I have to experience the fear that most of my clothes are missing. My bag never comes.

Fortunately I notice a tiny, little sign that says if your luggage came from a country not in the European Union, it's at Carousel #28.

Now I have to decide whether the United States is a member of The European Union, or not. Not knowing what the European Union even is, and really having no other choice, I run to Carousel #28 to find an entire room of luggage standing around, probably belonging to people who didn't see that tiny little sign.

Amazingly I find my bag, and have the urge to drop to my knees and kiss it, but I overcome that urge, because strange behavior in airports is not lightly tolerated anymore. I go to leave and I'm stopped by Security and told I must have my bag X-rayed.

To show you how deeply engrained these kinds of traumatic events are, sitting at my desk and writing this 12 years later, I can still feel the tension and the relief of seeing my bag in Carousel #28 and I can still see it in my mind.

I pass the X-ray with flying colors, explaining my dental instruments once again, and hurry upstairs to grab a cab to Marbella. The line for cabs is a block long, and no one seems to know how far away Marbella actually is.

Estimates range up to an hour and a cost of 80 Euros. Suddenly a bus pulls in marked Marbella, and without asking anyone I jump on.

Well, ... not exactly. First I have to undo my luggage cart that keeps tipping over, put my bags in the bus' luggage space under the bus, and lug my heavy camera bag onto the bus.

I ask the bus driver in Spanish if he stops at the El Fuerte Miramar, and he told me he stops at the El Fuerte, but not the El Fuerte Miramar, but not to worry because it's "close."

I'm hot and exhausted from the stress of feeling like I lost my luggage twice in one morning, and from running to make connections, and from the fact that I'm still wearing my sport jacket which doubles as my passport holder because I'm afraid that if I take it off, I'm sure I will lose something important, so I leave it on.

It's ninety degrees, and I'm wearing a jacket, and lugging a heavy bag and the rest of my belongings. However, it turns out that despite my excellent Spanish, the bus driver didn't understand me, because he wasn't going anywhere near the hotels.

When he gets to Marbella, he pulls into a bus depot, and everyone has to get out. Trip's over. That's as far as he goes. So once again, I'm forced to pack my horrible, wheeling, foldable luggage cart, with the stretched out elastic from just one day's use, and try to find a cab to my hotel.

I navigate outside the bus depot where I find a huge row of stairs, and no escalator. So just as I finished packing my luggage cart, I must once again unpack it, to hand carry all these things down the stairs. Still wearing my jacket of course.

Now I get to the bottom and find another long line for a taxi, but once again another bus, this time the #9 pulls in and that one goes to the hotels. Great, except that once again, I have to undo my luggage cart, and put my bags on the bus. I feel like I've been lifting weights in a winter coat for six hours.

On top of that the bus has only one narrow door, which I can hardly fit through with my carry on luggage. On buses in Spain, you pay according to how far you're going. The driver calculates it. It costs me about two Euros, ... well worth it, and this is the bus that takes me "near" to my hotel.

It didn't feel that near when I was navigating through the hot streets, but I finally make my grand entrance to the El Fuerte Miramar, not in a limo, or even a taxi, but by walking up to the hotel dragging heavy luggage that's turning over once every three minutes like clockwork. Very classy!!!

Two young kids are standing outside in uniform, but make no move to help me, until I request it in Spanish. I'm trying to navigate the curb to the hotel without my luggage falling over again, when in exasperation I ask for assistance.

I can't even bear to look at my luggage at this point, and I run into the lobby assuming they'll take care of it for me. I still have my heavy camera bag and my jacket.

It's now after 4 P.M., and I had visions of me being in the Marbella sun by 2. The girl at the desk speaks good English and checks me in to the smallest room I have ever seen, for 148 Euros a night. But it has a great bathroom. I'm so exhausted I don't even complain. The only thing I ask is why it's so dark.

In Spain, in 2008, in order to turn on the lights or the A.C. you had to put your hotel room card into a special slot that activates the electricity. If you take it out for any reason you're in the dark, with no air.

I don't even care anymore. All I want to do is to relax. I decided to get to the beach no matter what. I go to open my suitcase, and it won't unzip. No, I'm not kidding. It won't unzip. Somehow it had gotten damaged, maybe from when my jacket got caught, and the zipper wouldn't move past a certain spot.

After all I had gone through I couldn't get to my clothes or swimsuits.

I tried my best to keep my composure, so I wouldn't look at this as a sign that I should have stayed home. I took a nail clipper, and all of my dental skills, plus a few prayers, and worked on that zipper until I got it to open. I can still feel the feeling of relief.

I hit the beach at the "perfect" sunning time of 5 P.M. and it was still hard to get a chair or towels. This hotel runs out of towels every few minutes. I learned to bring my own after the first day.

I just sat there until 6 P.M. and then tried to get dinner but the beach restaurant had just closed, so I ate my 15 Euro hamburger with a fried egg on top at the bar. I was so hungry I would have eaten sand, with a side order of suntan lotion at that point.

At least now I could rest. But I needed to find new luggage.

IN SEARCH OF LUGGAGE – AND THE CLUB SCENE IN MARBELLA

The search for new luggage was a priority, and since it stays light out in Spain until about 9:30 P.M., and stores stay open late, I felt I had plenty of time. My plan was to find new luggage, and then have some fun.

I went to the concierge to ask some questions about where I might find new luggage, when I met beautiful Virginia who was at a table in the lobby attempting to sell real estate.

She looked like a young Candy Bergen, (that kind of perfect nose), and she was so helpful to me. She actually drew maps for me, which I could not interpret because of my ADHD, but when a beautiful girl is taking the time to draw maps for you, you don't tell her you have ADHD and can't use them.

You do what I did, and make believe you couldn't have understood them any better had you been a famous cartographer.

Things were going great, until she mentioned her boyfriend, ... twice. That spurred me to leave and begin my quest for my new suitcase.

I was in a great hurry to find one, because my type of ADHD fills my head with the kind of fears that tell me that I won't find any luggage in time for my next flight, and that I'll either lose all of my clothing as a result of that, or that I'll have to try and carry armfuls of clothing by hand through the airport, and on to Barcelona.

I finally find a store where they happily rip me off for a bag costing 40 Euros, (about $51. U.S. at that time), but the bag turns out to be defective. Unfortunately I find out too late, ... while I'm on my way to Barcelona. Not only did the zipper break, but the wheels fell off, and I had to literally drag it through the streets.

I wound up re-buying the same bag in Barcelona for only 15 Euros, which was probably still too much. It should run from their noses! (Which is an old expression my grandmother used to say! LOL)

On the way back to my hotel with the new piece of luggage, I pass a Vodaphone store where a nice, helpful guy worked feverishly for about an hour, but to no avail, to try and get me a SIM card for my European telephone that had an expired Swiss SIM card.

Nothing worked, and after an hour, I leave, thanking him profusely for his time. At least I got the luggage, but I feel partially naked without a working cell phone, as in New York, I often walk with it in my hand. Even in those days!

I finally hit the shower around 11 P.M., and by midnight, I'm ready to hit the Marbella club scene in Puerto Banus. As a long time, card carrying member of the New York nightclub scene, I figured this would be a snap.

Plus I was coming with an introduction from one of New York's pre-eminent club impresarios my dear friend Michael Ault, who had owned, and originally opened the Pangaea nightclub in Marbella.

He gave me the name of the current owner, a man named Markus, and told me to introduce myself. That's usually all you need to open doors on the club scene, a really powerful name as an introduction.

Unless my cab driver was trying to get off easy by leaving me a few blocks away, which I don't think he was, it seems that cabs can't enter the yacht area of Puerto Banus where the club is located, only Rolls Royces, Ferrari's, Benz's and the like.

My kind of scene. It made me wonder if my new white pimped-out Jag would have been allowed in, because I didn't notice any lowly Jaguars.

I approached the bouncers at the door, (they even had a velvet rope), and asked for Markus. This handsome, huge Black guy named Vaughn, with an English accent, told me that Markus was in Sweden, but just on the strength of his name, I was ushered into the club, (for free of course!).

I was then taken to Diane, the girl who was in charge of admitting people, who was told that I was a friend of the owner, and that I was "cool". It's the same all over the world. If you're cool in New York, you're cool wherever you go! (LOL) It's always who you know.

I expected a resort type club filled with hip, beautiful tourists, and people who would invite me onto their yachts. Instead I felt like I had walked into a private party, to which I wasn't invited, magnified by the fact that I don't drink alcohol, and that in New York, I'm usually known wherever I go, and always have someone to talk to.

Here, I leaned on various walls, struck different poses to make it look like I was comfortable, and basically wandered around the room feeling like a transplanted farmer from Idaho, who suddenly found himself at a hip Hollywood party.

They were all regulars who knew each other. I didn't know that people actually lived in Marbella. I thought it was only a tourist spot for the rich and fabulous.

I found an empty banquette where I sat for about an hour nursing my ice-cold cranberry juice, until someone told me that it was reserved, for a late coming party, and asked me to move.

I would have left earlier, but when someone is kind enough to let me into a club for free, and treats me so graciously, I always feel it's a snub if I leave right away.

I did what I do in New York. I made believe someone had called me and asked me to meet them somewhere else. Both Diane and Vaughn told me to come back anytime, and that I was always welcome.

They were both really nice, as was the pretty girl who just walked up to me at the bar and kissed me on the lips. I never asked her why, or if she thought she knew me. It was just enough that she did it.

I found a McDonald's, (in Marbella???), had a snack, endured some snide comments from a bunch of drunken guys I passed in the street, and then had two cute girls walking towards me address me in Spanish.

I speak Spanish, but didn't understand what they said. I asked them in English, and they said they thought I looked "cool", and that they liked "my look." A welcome change from the negative remarks from the obviously jealous drunks just moments before.

I had to find a cab to take me back to my hotel. The girls took me to a cab stand, which was in the opposite direction from where I was wandering, because in Marbella, you can't just hail a cab like you do in New York. You can only get them at cab stands.

This one girl, (the hotter of the two), actually ran out into traffic to grab me one, and I'm sure the cabby only stopped because she was so pretty, and he thought that she was going to be the passenger. Instead he wound up with me.

In Marbella cabs have no meter. You tell them where you're going, and they look up the charge. My trip cost me 11.9 Euros, and you don't have to tip, but I did out of habit. I got to bed around 3 A.M. and requested a 9:30 wake-up call.

After all, I didn't come to Marbella to sleep.

MARBELLA - DAY 2

Day two in Marbella, my wake-up call comes at 9:30. It's not a call, just a series of beeps, but it works. All of my hotels include breakfast, which is a wonderful thing, to not have to search out a place to eat in the morning. That is one thing I will always remember to ask for when I'm traveling, a hotel that gives you breakfast.

I drag my butt downstairs to find a long line for breakfast, but I'm in by 10 A.M., and it's definitely worth the wait. It's a huge buffet with tons of food, and they even make you custom eggs. I had my eggs "vuelta y vuelta" which I believe is the way you say, "Over easy." Unfortunately I had wanted them over medium, but this was okay too.

The breakfast room opens onto the pool, but when I go out there, they've already run out of towels, and won't have any for about half an hour, so I go back up to my room to write my travel notes. Those notes came in very handy when writing this book. Someone who read an early draft commented on my amazing memory! (LOL)

I go back to the pool around 12:15 with towels from my room just in case, but the sun is too hot on my faux-tanned skin, so I sit in the shade and study Italian to prepare for the second leg of my trip, then go back upstairs and fall asleep until about 3 P.M.

In Spain that still leaves plenty of time to do things since as I mentioned, it stays light out until 9:30 P.M.

I take a bus to Puerto Banus for 1.15 Euros, instead of the 12 Euros by cab, and when I get there, I shop at the myriad of booths and stalls, and buy cool presents for family and people back home.

I eat Paella with seafood, which was delicious, find a phone store where they hook me up with the correct SIM card for Spain, and mistakenly think it would work with the 6 Euro pre-paid phone card I had bought that gave me about 800 minutes to call the USA.

After calling my Mom, my daughter Liz, and my best friend Todd, I run out of money on my SIM card. Surprise! It doesn't use the cheap minutes on the calling card. It uses it's own more expensive minutes, which was a good lesson for me.

I also learned that the country code for Spain is 034, the US is 001, and Europe is 011 to dial from the States. I had never made a trans-Atlantic call before in my entire sheltered life.

I found what is known as a "locutorio", which are amazing little rooms with telephones that you can use to call the United States for only 10 cents a minute.

I wind up spending a lot of time in those hot little rooms, as I searched them out in Barcelona, and also in Italy, where they don't seem to be as numerous as they are in Spain.

I take lots of digital photos of all the amazing yachts, and I wander around Puerto Banus until around 10:30 at night.

I'm back in my room by 11:30 ready to get some sleep and get an early start on my last full day in Marbella. I finally get to bed by 1 A.M.

MARBELLA/PUERTO BANUS - DAY 3

I get up at 8 A.M., grab two towels from my room, and run to the beach to get two lounges. I am determined to get some Marbella beach sun. Believe it or not, even at that ungodly hour, all of the thatched-umbrella chairs are already taken. I pull two chairs over to the side, making believe I was waiting for a friend, but truthfully am planning on using the extra one to invite some lucky girl to join me! (LOL)

By 12:30, my skin is burning, and I'm alone, and rather than try and sell the chairs, which I probably could have done, I approach two girls from England, and offer the chairs to them. It was a bit awkward because they were both topless as most of the women were on the beaches, but in Europe it's expected.

That's when I came to the conclusion that European men are all geniuses.

Somehow they figured out a way to convince European women that they could go to the beach topless and no one would notice! And European women believed them! (LOL) Pure genius!!!

They were just lying on towels on the sand, and being from New York, and not used to topless women on the beach, I didn't know where to look as I addressed them. It felt very awkward to tell you the truth.

They were very grateful for the chairs and both jumped up and gave me big hugs which was even more awkward. One especially was a tall, thin model-type, and ordinarily when I meet nice people while traveling I ask to take a photo with them. In this case I decided against it! (LOL)

During my stay on the beach, I discover a guy I had been looking for for years. A guy to star in the film I've been wanting to shoot called "Men Who Exercise in Inappropriate Places", about a guy who exercises anywhere but the gym.

On line at the post office, maybe at the bank, and even at the beach where other people are trying to relax and get some sun.

You've heard of Jack La Lanne? Well this was Jack La Lunatic, and I managed to get him on film. He was literally right next to me, and I positioned my camera on my blanket in a way to film him surreptitiously as he made a fool of himself, doing calisthenics on the sand.

He was with a woman and it looked like he was doing this to try and impress her, but she acted as if she didn't even notice. He insisted on doing all kinds of crunches where he moved his legs in a "double butterfly" type of movement.

He was hilarious, and didn't even have good abs. He probably only exercises this way on the beach in front of strangers, because if he had done what he did on the beach on a regular basis at the gym, he'd have a rock-hard six-pack.

At 1:30 I'm ready to go out exploring. I decide to start out in the neighborhood. Not realizing that most of the stores are closed on Sunday, I went to an empty shopping district.

Then I go to Opencor, a huge convenience store chain, find a "locutorio" that I could use later, and chat up a girl named Jenny, who worked there and wore a skirt so short, she wouldn't have had to get undressed for a gynecologist appointment.

I leave and find some little beautiques that were open and buy more presents. Then I discover an amazing boardwalk running along the beach, that had millions of tourist-trap stores, and they were all open.

I walk until I think I have discovered an amazing bargain, a tour on a child-like choo-choo train-car that winds through the city streets for only 5 Euros. I buy a ticket and hop on. It turns into a comedy sketch. The tour guide never says ONE WORD!!!

The entire half hour trip, he just drives, and never addresses the crowd, or tells us where we're going or what we're seeing. He doesn't even have a microphone hooked up.

I keep waiting for him to begin speaking, but as he pulls back in to the place where we started, and no one on the "tour" had any idea of where we had been, I realized the humor of the situation. Not one word did this man utter!

You go on a tour where the guide never speaks to you, never tells you what you're seeing or where you are, and then he just drives you back. It was a drive that billed itself as a tour. No wonder it was only five Euros. Any more than that and people would probably complain, and beat the guy. For five Euros they accepted it.

I try to find my way back to where I started, but my ADHD kicks in and I'm totally lost. Fortunately I wasn't hungry, but I definitely need a Men's Room.

I'm trying to remember signposts, but I'm not able to, and just when I think I'm definitely lost, I recognize that somehow I had walked in a circle, and I'm actually back at my own hotel. I still don't know how that happened. Thank G-d I recognized it.

I get to use my own bathroom, drop off the presents I had bought, and then I go back out to try and find that "locutorio" I had located.

No one I called was home. Not one person except a friend of mine whose life wasn't going that well, and she decides to try and tell me every single depressing story in detail, until I have to remind her that I'm in Spain, and have to go.

I have my heart set on one more Paella with seafood, but I'm not able to find any that looked like the one I had gotten in Puerto Banus, so at around 7:30 P.M. I board a bus headed towards Puerto Banus.

It wasn't the one I was supposed to take, but it came, and when I ask the bus driver where it went, he says he doesn't stop at Corte Ingles, where I'm supposed to go, but he stops near enough that it would be okay. All this in Spanish mind you. Unbeknownst to me, trouble lies ahead!

I don't know if it was my ADHD, or the sleep disorder I battle, but I must have fallen asleep on the bus. Suddenly I wake up with a start, and just have this feeling that I had passed my stop.

I ask the driver, and he seems annoyed. The stop we just passed was my stop. He claims that he yelled out the stop, and I didn't hear him. In either case it was too late. He tells me I'd have to stay on the bus until he got back to the beginning of the route and start over again.

It's funny, but sometimes when I go into this kind of "dream" state, which I think is what must have happened, I think I'm still awake and that I know what's going on.

So in my dream state, I hazily recalled sleeping through only one stop, and figured I would just walk back to where I was supposed to be. After all, how far away could one stop be? I was to learn exactly how far in the next few minutes.

I convince the driver to let me off the bus at the next stop. He doesn't try and stop me, and he doesn't tell me how far away I was. I must have been about 3 miles away from my destination.

Not knowing this, I begin walking, ... and walking, ... and walking. Finally I get up the nerve to ask a woman I saw how far I was from Puerto Banus, and she just looks at me and says, "Muy lejos" (Very far.)"

I find myself walking until the road ended and became a highway. Then I'm walking on the grass alongside the highway. I'm trying my best to stay calm, because getting lost is one of my worst fears. Especially in another country!

I'm also trying not to berate myself for falling asleep on the bus, and missing my stop and getting myself into this situation in the first place.

I make a mental note to call the sleep center when I get back to ask for new medication. All of a sudden I come upon an accident that looked like it had just happened moments before.

A guy who had been on a motorcycle must have collided with a car, and is lying in the middle of the road. Traffic immediately backed up for miles behind him.

I want to take a film of it because I have my video camera, but I know I didn't really want to see it. And I didn't want the injured guy to see me taking the film.

The guy looks like he'll be fine, but they were waiting for an ambulance, and no one could pass the scene, so traffic was just backed up for miles, and as I keep walking, it sort of becomes my job to tell people stuck in their cars what had happened.

The problem is I have to tell them in Spanish, because in Spain people take it for granted that you speak Spanish, especially if you are wandering along the highway. So suddenly I'm transformed into a Spanish traffic reporter.

When I finally reach Puerto Banus, I could see the place I was trying to get to. The only problem is that it's on the other side of the highway, and cars are going around 70 miles an hour. Not a good place to cross.

However, my ADHD tells me that maybe I could make it, because otherwise I will have to spend the rest of my life on this side of the highway.

Fortunately, I have learned not to accept the fear that my subconscious mind creates, and I reject the plan of trying to run across the highway.

I had read many stories of people who had been killed that way, and it would really be too stupid if that happened to me, especially while I was away on vacation.

So I ask The Universe for wisdom, and then it comes to me. I backtrack a little bit to where the Puerto Banus sign was, and find an offshoot of the highway. A lady is walking with a little boy about a block away, and I get her attention.

She speaks no English, but I make myself understood, and as luck would have it, she is going to the exact same place that I am trying to get to. She tells me to follow her.

She leads me to an underpass that takes me out on the other side of the highway, exactly where I had been trying to go. It was now after 9 P.M., but it was still light out. I'm right at the marketplace I had been trying to find.

I go right to the belt stand, buy two belts, two pair of drawstring pants from a girl named Miriam, take a couple of photos with her because she was so cute, then get the Paella I had been thinking about all day, and everything was good again.

Around 10:05, I plan to go back to my room, pack, and study some Italian phrases I was trying to learn for the Italian part of my trip. I run to the bus stop, and just catch the bus as it was getting ready to leave.

I get on right in back of a beautiful blonde woman in a very short skirt, and a gorgeous golden tan. She seemed very unfriendly, so that was my challenge. Half an hour later, we were back at my hotel enjoying a Flamenco dance troupe.

Originally from Brazil, she had been living in Marbella for about seven months. She had literally just come off the beach when she met me, and she kept apologizing for her appearance, which honestly couldn't have been better.

Some women would need hours to look that good. She had a few drinks, which unfortunately affected her badly, and she began crying that she would never find a man that loved her for who she was, and didn't just want her for her body.

Unfortunately I could not be that man, so by the time she left, it was after 2 A.M., and I still had to pack and be ready for a 7:30 wake-up call. Like many men, when beautiful women are around I seem to lose all track of time! On to Barcelona!

BARCELONA - DAY 1 - 8/21/06

With about 4 ½ hours sleep, I jump up ready to go when the phone rings at 7:30. I shower, enjoy my last outdoor breakfast, grab a couple of snacks for my travel bag, and run to catch the cab they called for me.

Francisco was right on time, in a brand new Mercedes, with great AC and relaxing music. A perfect trip, except that he gets me there so quickly, it's only 11 A.M, and my flight is at 2:30.

When I get out of his car, and he takes my bags out of his trunk, one of the things that only happens to me happened. Somehow, and it isn't even possible for this to happen, one of the elastic bands from my horrible luggage cart, managed to slip inside the metal pull of one of the zippers on my suitcase.

You would literally have to work for hours to get that to happen, if there was ever any reason in the world you wanted to, but when I travel, things like that happen to me routinely.

I was ready to cut it, out of frustration, and ruin the cart, but he actually managed to free it.

He charged me 62 Euros. I gave him 65, and he was very happy. I was glad I was there early, until I went inside to check in at Spanair.

I have a 2:30 flight to Barcelona, but because of all the hassles at the first airport, I wanted to be early. Except now I'm too early.

Spanair didn't allow check in until 12:30, so I take a seat, eat the apple I took from the Miramar Hotel where I had been staying, and around 12:15 I join a line that was already getting kind of long.

I finally check in around 1:15, and arrive at my gate at 1:30. Security in Europe is much easier than in the US.

It was a quick 90 minute flight, and I get to Barcelona around 4:30 as planned. My bag comes pretty quickly this time.

I jump right into a cab, whose driver estimated the cost at 18 Euros and he was right on the button. Despite the fact that I was told tipping isn't necessary, I'm too used to it not to do it, and they really appreciate the extra two Euros I add on.

The Hotel Regina was very nice. The room was small, but it had a nice bath, and I thought it was fine. It also had a nice writing table, and a beautiful lobby, with breakfast included of course.

I get up the courage and take the Metro to another part of town to attend a Spiritual meeting I had heard about. At that meeting, a fellow sitting next to me named Rob, who was from Australia of all places, tells the people in the room about a book he recently read that changed his life.

It just so happens that that very book was written by a good friend of mine back in New York. That can't even happen. I had the author's number he mentioned in my cell phone. That's how well I knew him.

Another guy at this same meeting, (and there were only about 8 of us), happened to be a sword swallower, and knew another friend of mine in New York, who's considered to be the ultimate superstar of sword swallowing. Go figure.

Out of eight guys across the world, I had friends in common with two of them. That's 25%. Again, not even possible. But a good sign!

BARCELONA - DAY 2 - 8/22/06

What I'm going to tell you next is a great example of my ADHD and the level of confusion I face. When I checked in the day before, I had mentioned that my room was nice, just a little small.

When I wake up the next morning, and go to look out the window to see what the weather was like, I wasn't able to do so, because I realize that my room has no windows. Not one window in the entire place. I hadn't noticed that small fact when I checked in.

I had set the alarm for 7:45, but allowed myself to sleep until 10, just because I needed it. I had planned on doing a morning tour at 9:30, and had requested a 7:45 A.M. wake-up call, but I had the feeling I really needed some rest, so I took the call, but went back to sleep for some well needed rest.

When I awoke, something seemed off slightly. Like the room seemed kind of dark. That's when it occurred to me after a brief search, that they had given me a room without windows.

It was basically a cave. I freaked out, because when I confirmed my reservation from the States, I had actually asked for a room with a view.

This room had a view, but it was a view of the furniture in the room. I shower, and I'm on my way down to breakfast, wondering if they were going to serve me food with no plates or silverware, when I see a maid cleaning another room.

I go in to ask for extra towels, and I'm both amazed and horrified to see that this room has floor to ceiling windows leading out to a balcony from which you could actually see the Plaza de Catalunya, which was only a couple of blocks away.

So I confronted the fear of changing rooms after I had unpacked all of my things, and I go to the desk and request a room change to the room I had seen. My other fear was that by changing rooms I would lose something, or leave something in the old room that I needed. Fear must be confronted in order to conquer it.

But I did it! I switch rooms right after breakfast, across the hall to room 207, and it was only around 12:30 P.M. I move all of my stuff, no problem and felt very proud of myself for doing so. Another fear confronted!

I figured I would sign up for a tour during the afternoon, and I would spend the next few hours exploring the area known as Las Ramblas on my own, as I had heard so much about it.

By 1:45, 45 minutes later, I'm still fumbling with the room safe, and I can't get it to work. It's a separate key, and I have experience with that from my stay at The Four Seasons in NYC, but I can't get it to work, and I'm wasting the whole day in my room.

I finally get a service guy to come up, and he fiddles around and says it's working fine now and is actually ready to leave, when I insist that he tries it again, and lo and behold, it doesn't work for him either. It was a good thing I asked him to stay for a minute. (Confronting the fear of feeling like you're imposing on someone!)

He calls a second genius, who decides that the battery is no good, and goes to get another one, which I think he kept in New York. Some thirty minutes later he finally returns, changes the battery, and finally I'm ready to hit the streets of Barcelona.

I had signed up for a tour at 15:30, (3:30 P.M. for you Americans!), and they only took cash, and I only had my credit card, so she trusted me to pay her later.

I go across the street to cash some Travelers Checks. The security in European banks is very tight. They X-ray all of your bags, and they only give you $200. maximum at a time.

I'm not sure what the purpose of that rule is, as if you need $300. or more to be a terrorist.

But you had to have your passport, and of course I didn't have mine, so I had to go back to my room to get it, and go back to that safe, and hope that it worked.

I actually found a Citibank in the area, which should theoretically have made things easier for me, since I'm a client, but of course it didn't. They closed at 2 P.M. I planned to go back the next day, but I did manage to check my account at an

ATM, and discovered to my horror that they had me down for only having $8.00 in assets. That's right, 8 whole dollars!

Absurd but perfect. Of all of my accounts holding many, many dollars they chose two tiny accounts to link to. One was a checking account that I thought I had closed years ago that showed a $2. balance, and then there was an old savings account that showed a grand total of $6.

What if anyone had checked my credit while I was there, in case I had to buy something expensive? They would have been very impressed to see that I was worth less than ten dollars. Thanks to my bank Citibank.

It takes almost an hour at the bank the next day to get that all sorted out, and to have two proper accounts replacing those two ridiculous accounts.

I asked them, of all of my accounts that they could have chosen, what in the world would make them choose those two. How idiotic!

Anyway, I go to find the tour place, and when I get there it's only 2:30 P.M., so I have an hour to waste. I find a little place near the tour office that had the worst hamburger I ever tasted.

And the so-called "fried potatoes" were like little raw lumps of something or other, that they kept on a plate and cooked until they looked exactly the same. I don't know how they did it, but they looked and tasted completely uncooked.

The tour was actually better than I had expected. It was a Tuesday, and not enough people had signed up so they combined us with another tour, and then the bus was pretty full by the time I got on.

They take us to the Park Guell that was built by Gaudi as were so many other things in Barcelona. He was like the Salvador Dali of Architecture, and his designs were amazing.

Somehow I manage to lose my tour group for a few minutes, and felt a little nervous because no one had our names or knew who we were, and I had no idea where I was or how I'd get home if I couldn't find the group. FEAR!

Suddenly I notice this huge guy from my bus, named Bernd, who was about 6'5", and could see over the crowds, and he recognized me as a fellow tourist and was nice enough to find our tour guide Pedro for me.

The last stop on the tour was the Picasso Museum, and then they drove us back to our starting point, but instead of taking us all the way back, they left us off a few blocks away.

This worked to my advantage because while finding my way back, I finally found a locutorio, which are those places where you can make calls to anywhere in the world for a small amount of money per minute.

That's where I meet the beautiful Lina from Sweden, who was working there behind the counter. She was amazing, and we bonded immediately. I took photos of her, and we hung out, until she too started telling me about her boyfriend, and I had to leave.

I drag myself away from Lina just before 8 P.M. and get back on a train to go to another one of those Spiritual meetings. Afterwards about six guys and I go out for a bite to eat, and one of them was nice enough to guide me back to the train, so I could get back to my hotel. Luckily that seems to happen to me just when I need it. I always seem to be surrounded by angels! (Like the two on my book cover! LOL)

Look at me. I'm in Spain, all alone, traveling by subway, and it's all good. I get back to the Plaza de Catalunya around 11 P.M. and the place is packed with tourists.

I go to sit down on a bench, thinking I'd study some Italian in preparation for my visit to Italy, and almost as soon as I sit down I'm joined by a creature of the night, who sits a little too close to me, and looked like he was up to no good.

Not worrying whether I would embarrass him or not, I grab my things and literally jump up, and head right back to my room.

I spend the rest of the night logging in my videotapes, and writing notes for my journal. One more day in Barcelona, then off to Italy.

BARCELONA - DAY 3 - 8/23/06

It's Wed., 8/23/06, and I sleep until 9 A.M. No wake-up call. I have breakfast around 10:15, and it was much more crowded today. I do what I had been doing, and pack a couple of tiny sandwiches and a few small cakes in some napkins to take with me to nibble on during the day.

I get to Citibank early assuming that things would be easier since I was a Citibank customer for the last 25 years or so, and I have my Gold Card with me. Boy was I wrong.

It seems that banks in Europe do not honor the Gold Cards from The United States. So where the other bank I went to, where I was a total stranger, charged me a total of 6 Euros commission to cash my Travelers Checks, my own bank where I had been a loyal customer for 25 years, only wanted to charge me 12 Euros! Great to go to your own bank! Not!!!

With the help of a girl who spoke English, I call the international number, and get a guy named Ron in India who tries to help me. He switches my linked savings account to an account that shows a lot more than six dollars, but he can't switch my checking account.

For that, he says he has to switch me to someone in the Citi Gold department. I almost lose it, but somehow I manage to stay calm. I try asking him, how I was supposed to draw cash if I needed it, if Citibank chose to show I only had eight dollars.

Where was the logic in that? What possible sense does that make for my own bank to choose the two smallest, most insignificant amounts of money to show for me? Homeless people had more money in their accounts than I did.

I refuse to pay Citibank twice what I paid at the other bank, so I leave and go back to the strange bank where they treated me much better. I get my cash and hit Las Ramblas where I find a few good bargains. I buy about 5 carry bags in bright, happy colors, and about 8 T-shirts for a total sum of about $57. That was cool.

One story I forgot to tell and I don't recall which day it was when I was in Spain, but it was definitely another fear of mine. I got locked inside a bathroom in Spain in a rarely used corridor, until someone discovered me and managed to get me out.

Luckily I had already ordered food at a restaurant counter, and asked the woman behind the counter where the rest room was. It was through a doorway and down a long corridor where there was nothing else. It was totally secluded.

As I entered the rest room I was standing in front of the toilet when the lights suddenly went out and I was in total darkness. I tried the door handle and it wouldn't open. I was stuck in the bathroom in total darkness far from anyone who could hear me yelling, ... and I was yelling!

I brought up my martial arts skills and started karate-kicking the door to no avail. I'm yelling out for help and it felt like I was in there for a long time, when the waitress realized I hadn't come back and thankfully sent someone to look for me.

That guy was somehow able to unlock the door and get me out. Thank G-d I had already ordered food or else I might still be in there. Another horrible experience ending in a miracle. I made sure to leave her a big tip!

Another great thing that happened while I was on Las Ramblas. I struck up a conversation with a beautiful girl riding a bicycle who happened to be a singer named Nikol Kollars. In talking, the subject of comedy came up and she asked me if I happened to know a comedian in the U.S. named Reggie Watts. I did not at the time. He was not famous yet! He's currently the band leader for The Late, Late Show with James Corden!

I get back to the States and attend the Andy Kaufman Award comedy contest at Carolines Comedy Club, and who was the winner but Reggie Watts. Amazing! I went back to introduce myself to him and write about his big win and we've been friends ever since!

FROM SPAIN TO ITALY - 8/24/06

It's Thursday, 8/24/06, and I get my wake-up call at 6:30 A.M. The nervousness of traveling day was right there laying next to me as I awoke.

I go into the bathroom to wash up, only to find another one of those unusual things that only happens to me. One of my bath towels had fallen and was draped across the open toilet.

It didn't fall into the toilet. It was just laying across it, which was basically the same thing to me. I wouldn't use it. Fortunately I had others.

Even more important, as I was packing the night before, I noticed that my brand new piece of luggage, turned out to be more like a piece of you know what. It was already broken, and the screws that held the wheels on were falling out.

Of course no one at the desk could fix it, but they promised me that the man who could fix it would come to my room by 8 A.M.

By 8:30 A.M. I'm still waiting. He shows up at 8:40. I had told them to tell him to bring screws, but like all men who fix things all over the world, he was unprepared.

He has no screws, but he tries to take the screws out of my luggage to use as examples, which would have made my problem even worse. Knowing this, I stop him cold, and tell him to go and get an assortment of screws, and we'd see which one fits.

He was just like the handymen in this country who invariably make the problem worse before they make it better, ... if you're lucky. I'm usually not.

And they just keep saying "No problem" when you tell them what you need them to do even though it usually winds up a HUGE problem.

Most of the time I wind up worse off afterwards than I was before. Maybe that's just my luck with repairmen and contractors. Who knows?

He's not able to find the right screw, so I give him permission to take a really long screw and screw it through the entire bag hoping that it would hold. It does, but only for about 30 minutes, which was just enough time to get nowhere.

A bellboy helps me down to the lobby to wait for my cab, and because I was using that crummy luggage cart on wheels that I got in Home Depot before I left, my bags were not well balanced on each other and just kept tipping over.

Nowhere during any of my travels did I see one other person whose luggage kept tipping over, and falling all over the ground. Not one person in any of the places I went and with all the people I saw in the airports. No one travels with the lack of grace that I travel with, and it's all through no fault of my own. I manifest it through my fears.

No matter how I set up my luggage, it never fits anywhere. It certainly never fits down the aisles of the airplane, so I'm always twisting my back to try and carry my garment bag, my carry-on bag, and my fold-up luggage cart on wheels through the narrow aisles, while trying not to hit the passengers in their seats as I pass by.

Then when I get to my row, I have to put all of my stuff down, and try and get it into the overhead. I can never take the chance to check all of my clothing, because as I explained in case they lose it, I'm not able to buy clothing off the rack. I can't just walk in anywhere and expect to be able to buy a new wardrobe. So I must carry a garment bag with me wherever I go.

Anyway, I have my last breakfast at The Hotel Regina, and grab a few tea sandwiches and some small cakes for the airport. Then just before my cab arrives, my ADHD tells me to run back to my room to check it one more time to make sure I didn't leave anything, and when I come back down, I accidentally get into the service elevator instead of the guest elevator, and when it reaches the lobby I can't figure out how to get out.

There was a lever for the door that I didn't know about and I had to bang on the elevator door for someone to come over and let me out.

My bags didn't even fit through my hotel room door, or down the hallways. I had to unload the cart and carry everything by hand. Very comfortable.

So the cab shows up. My driver was Raquel, a nice girl who really didn't speak much English. I make a mental note to request a driver who speaks English next time, especially in Italy.

When I'm tired or tense, it's hard for me to speak Spanish, so this long conversation with Stephanie is giving me a headache. I realize I must be in really great physical shape if talking gives me a headache.

For some reason it only cost me 18 Euros to get from the airport to my hotel, but from the hotel back to the airport cost me 30 Euros. There's always some excuse that's hard to understand, usually having something to do with the luggage, the time of the month, and the angle of the sun.

I have to get to Alitalia Airlines. Raquel was not able to drop me off right in front, so she lets me off where I have to maneuver two high curbs while doing my luggage balancing act just to get inside the terminal. Then the fun really begins.

I go to the Information desk, and the woman there tells me that Alitalia was on lines 10 and 11. I wait on line 11, but after a while I find out I'm on the wrong line. I'm supposed to be on lines 13 and 14, and by now they are both long lines. What a surprise!

I want to go back to the woman who told me 10 and 11, and force her to explain her ignorance, but of course I don't because these days you can not start any commotion in the airport, or you'll find yourself under arrest.

Finally I get to check my bag, but they don't have identifying tags to fill out. They only have stickers. Fine. I'll use stickers.

I get through security, and go to my gate, and I realize I have time to get a bite to eat. I go to the restaurant, which is bordered by metal poles spaced too close to each other to allow my luggage cart to roll between them.

So once again, I have to undo my luggage from the straps, take the whole thing apart, and make my way in, towards the only table I see available. Just before I get to it, some guy takes it. If I hadn't had to undo my entire luggage cart yet once again, I would have had the table. I'm starting to feel the stress building up again.

Now I had my luggage, but no table. A nice waitress sees my dilemma, and leads me to a table that has no chair. So I'm standing by a table with my luggage while they search for a chair for me.

I'm finally seated and I order a tuna sandwich expecting something similar to what I've eaten all my life. They call it "atun", with the "a" in front instead of at the end, but it was supposed to be tuna. What came out was nothing like anything I had ever had before.

They brought me something on a roll that was all dry, crumbled, and falling out of the roll. No mayonnaise and chopped celery for these tuna lovers. It was like small pieces of dried sardines.

I take a few bites and take the rest with me. Ordinarily I would have just thrown it away, but you never know what you'd be willing to eat when you're starving.

We go to board the plane, and I wheel my luggage to the entrance door, when the Captain stops me and tells me my luggage is too big. Maybe it was the forlorn, beaten look on my face, but for some unknown reason he relents and lets me come on board.

He takes my luggage personally and stows it in a cabin upfront reserved for First Class passengers, saving me the hassle of getting it to my exit row, where I had requested to sit, as I always do when I fly.

My exit row is uncomfortable because the seats don't recline. I sit next to a guy named Mateo, who silently fights me for the common arm rest, and who I start out hating because he keeps banging into my arm, and never says "Excuse me."

I decide to try and let it go, and I begin a conversation with him. Turns out he's a nice guy on his way to Rome. We get friendly and he begins helping me with my Italian. His English is poor, but a lot better than my Italian, which is derived mostly from my knowledge of Spanish.

We land on time, around 1:30 P.M., and I have to catch the train to Florence at 2:55, so I feel like I have plenty of time to get to baggage claim, get my other suitcase, and then find the train.

I'm wheeling my garment bag and accessory bag on the cart, trying my best to keep it from tipping over, but to get to baggage claim I have to go up two staircases with no escalator, which means that each time I go up the stairs I have to undo my luggage cart, take off the bags, and carry three things up the stairs. Then at the top of the stairs I have to put it all back together again. It's exhausting to say the least.

I get my luggage fairly quickly, and that's when it all starts. Part of the bottom breaks off of my brand new suitcase, so now I'm the proud owner of a heavy suitcase with no wheels that won't fit onto my luggage cart because it's too big.

I want to run back to Barcelona and hit the guy in the head with it.

I have to get to Termini Station to catch the train, and some guy who works there tells me there was a train to take me there upstairs. "Real easy", he says. Just go through those doors and walk until you have holes in your shoes.

I go through the door where he directs me to go, and see nothing, and no one to ask. Most people don't speak English anyway. In the hotels they speak English, but not the average transit worker, which makes sense. Back in New York, how many of our transit workers are poly-linguists???

Finally I find a guy who sends me back into the terminal, to go upstairs across a bridge to the other side of the street. The escalators all have metal poles in front of them, and my luggage doesn't fit through, so once again, I have to take it all apart, and try my best to carry my cart, leather carry-on bag, my garment bag, and my large suitcase that can no longer stand up by itself because the wheels broke off.

I literally feel like killing myself. I'm so exhausted, and I have no idea how far I still am from my destination. All I know is that the hour and a half I had to get to my train is disappearing very quickly.

At the top of the escalator, I stop to rest, put my bags back onto the cart, and come to yet another escalator where I must go through the same thing yet again. My bags are falling all over, and people are looking at me with pity.

After balancing everything on one escalator, one woman calls out to me that something had fallen off my suitcase. It was the entire rest of the bottom structure where the wheels used to be. In order to go and get it I had to put my bags down and they all fell over, so there I am in a walkway with all of my stuff strewn all over.

All I could think of to do was take out my video camera and take a film of it. And in the midst of that some Italian putz comes by and complains, "Hey, this is a walkway", as if I had done it on purpose.

Finally I see the train to the train. This is the intermediate train that takes me to the real train that takes me to Florence. It's getting later and later. Now it's already after 2 P.M. and my real train leaves at 2:55.

I have to buy a ticket and it's 9.5 Euros. I buy the ticket and rush to the train. There's a big space between the train and the platform, and I almost fall in, trying to lift my heavy, unbalanced bags in the air.

My jacket is folded up into a compartment of my garment bag and will probably look like a used napkin when I take it out.

I finally manage to get on the train, and there's no room to sit. I'm almost grateful I can stand right near where I am by the door, when a few moments later a whole bunch of people push on, and even the standing area is now crowded.

The train finally leaves, and the trip to Termini Station is the longest trip known to man. At least it feels that way. The only advantage was that because of where I was standing with my bags, I was right next to the door when it finally arrived at Termini.

That didn't mean it was easy to get off, only that I was nearest to the door. However I had to figure out what to press to make the door open, while a whole car full of people waited to disembark.

Finally some kind person helped me out. How am I supposed to know how to operate trains in Rome? Now there was not only a big gap between the train and the station, but I also had to walk down a big step to get off.

I basically threw all my stuff out on the platform, and raced off to find the next train not knowing where I was going, just knowing I had only ten minutes left to find it.

I'm at the right station, but I have to find the right track number, and there's no one around to ask.

I begin to race down this long platform feeling the panic starting to build as I realize that I might miss my train, and who knows how long I'd have to wait for the next one.

I'm asking everyone I see, but as soon as I realize they don't speak English, I run away like a madman, with no time to be polite.

Finally one guy tells me I was going the right way, but then I see a group of Carabiniere, the Italian cops, and I ask them. They barely spoke English either, but I was able to make out their suggestion to look on the message boards, which were pre-printed, so I guess the trains always run on the same track.

I think I ran for half a mile or more. All I know is I was completely exhausted. I finally find a listing on the wall that said "Firenze" the Italian word for

Florence, but it did not have the same time listing as the one I was supposed to take.

It was the only one I saw so I decided to go for it, however I was at track #26, and it was on track #5.

I start to run, literally banging into people and yelling "Perdonne-mei" as I ran, fully expecting some guy to grab hold of me and start a fight.

I make it with barely two minutes to spare, and I jump onto the first car I see, because I have no time to search for the car I was assigned to.

It could have started pulling out, and I would have had to start chasing a train pulling my luggage behind me.

I jump the gap, and drag my bags up the three steps into the train. I have no way of knowing I had jumped onto the first class accommodations. I certainly would not have known by looking at them because they looked very ordinary, and had an aisle about six inches wide. Perfect if you're built like a snake. Most people are not.

I was ready to collapse in heat, pain, frustration, and exhaustion. I try to wheel my bags down the aisle, but they get stuck on literally every single seat. I finally manage to drag each bag to an empty seat, and as soon as I settle into it, some guy shows up and tells me it was his seat.

My ticket said Car #6, but there was no way I was going to try and drag all my stuff through five more long cars while they were moving, so I manage to find a seat in car #2 facing a strange foreign man wearing sandals exposing twisted, overlapping toes that I just had to take a picture of. That's how sick a state I was in, photographing some guy's deformed feet!

Oh, I left out one amazing thing that again could ONLY happen to me. I'm putting my luggage in a storage bin on the train between the cars, and there were only spaces on the top shelf.

I take my garment bag, lift it up as high as I can high, and throw it up on the shelf, but the shoulder strap was hanging down, and as I throw the bag, the shoulder strap loops itself over my head and pulls me off my feet into the luggage rack.

If anyone had seen that, they would have had to get hysterical laughing. Even I had to laugh despite the fact I had almost killed myself. The visual would have had to be amazing. It's being able to laugh at my ridiculous circumstances that keeps me going.

The conductor finally came through collecting tickets, and told me that I was in a first class seat.

He asked whether I wanted to move or pay the difference. I was prepared to pay up to an extra fifty dollars, just not to have to move again, so when he said it would cost me an extra $12.91, I thought he was kidding.

Then I realized that these men don't have much of a sense of humor, and don't go through the cars telling jokes, so I paid my $12.91, and stayed where I was.

I was just so exhausted. Fortunately, Firenze was to be the last stop, and I would have ten whole minutes to get my bags off the train. Because it was first class they served soda, with no ice, and salted crackers. I can only imagine what second class would have been like. They would probably have just served salt.

I just sat back, tried to relax, and thought about having to buy new luggage yet again, once I got to Florence. This time, I think I'll know what to look for.

I'm just starting to calm down, when I notice that it's almost 4:30 P.M., and time to continue the torture. The train comes in around 4:35, and it's just as I feared. It's three steps down, and a very narrow door, perfect for pulling a back muscle, as you try and twist your way through it holding your luggage.

Luggage thievery is very big in Italy, so I took the heaviest piece off first, thinking it would be the hardest to steal very quickly, as I ran back on for my other two pieces, while people tried to get off the train around me.

That's always the worst part. It would be bad enough if you were there all alone, but to have to struggle in front of groups of strangers who are always being held up by your situation, is a whole other story.

When all three pieces were on the platform, I had to take out my video camera and film how far I was going to have to walk, because it was absolutely ridiculous. There are no porters to help you, and even if there were, they wouldn't be able to speak English anyway.

It looked like I had to walk back to the United States. I finally found someone who spoke enough English to tell me I had to go all the way to the other end of the platform. I am now officially the "foreign man" I've been joking about for my whole entire life. (Inside joke!)

I finally reach the other end of the platform, and ask the taxi guy in Italian, how much to go to the Hotel Brunelleschi, and he tells me whatever is on the meter. The meter reads $7.30, but he added charges on for my bags that brought it to 11.

I check in and have my bags with me. I'm standing in front of an open elevator, waiting for it to come. For some reason, I could not tell that it was open, until a woman yelled out to me, "The elevator is open. Step in."

My room was small again, but at least this time it had a window. It also had a great bathroom, and was right in the heart of the action.

I did what I often do when I have some time. I walked the path of a place I had to go the next day, just to see if I could find it and make it easier to get to when I really had to go. Then I found another "locutorio". Those places are blessings. I called family and friends.

Then I came back to have dinner, and wound up eating in an empty dining room except for one couple. Needless to say the Maitre-d' was very attentive, as he had nothing else to do. He happened to be from Montreal, and spoke perfect English, so he gave me guidance on where to go.

It didn't make sense to me to go to sleep, so I walked down to the square, found the Ponte Vecchio, Uffizi Gallery, the statue garden, got ice cream, and walked across the Ponte Vecchio to try and find the Pitti Palace.

As usual, I followed the signs but they did not lead me to where I was going. I'm kind of used to it already, after all these years. I have the kind of ADHD where it affects my sense of direction, and my ability to follow instructions.

On the way back I meet a beautiful Albanian girl walking her dog. We speak for quite a while, and exchange numbers promising to get together, although I think both of us know it wasn't going to happen. It almost never does.

FLORENCE, ITALY - DAY 1 - 8/25/06

I sleep until 9 A.M. even though my wake-up call was for 8:30. I go for breakfast and come back to find that the maid had draped my shower mat across the bidet. Why she would do something like that was beyond me. Even though only the soles of my feet would touch it, would I want it touching something like a bidet?

It was definitely on a par with my towel falling across the open toilet the day before. Luckily for me, the maid spoke Spanish, and I asked her to change it for me. She couldn't understand why. I wouldn't want to eat dinner at her house!

I had signed up for a tour at 2:30, and decided to walk to the station just to make sure I knew where it was. I stopped in many stores along the way, and many interesting sites, and I easily found the corner where we were to meet.

I even found a replacement suitcase once again from a guy at a stand who spoke more Chinese than English. He wanted 20 Euros for it, and remembering my rip-off at 40 Euros, I talk him down to 16, only to find when I get it back to my room that it was way too big.

I bring it back to return it, thinking if I got the big one for 16 Euros, I could get the small one for maybe 12. My mistake. Once you own something you have very little bargaining power. He only returned 1 Euro to me, and I couldn't argue, but it sure beat the 40 Euro one that fell apart within minutes of using it. I will definitely cancel the payment on that when I get home.

Plus, the new suitcase is red and blue, which should make it very easy to spot. I had about 90 minutes to waste before my tour, so I wheeled the suitcase back to my hotel, and on the way back met the amazing Hella from Finland who lives here in Florence. She was tall, blonde, and beautiful, which didn't deter me from being friendly to her!

She spoke great English, and was kind enough to guide me back to my hotel. She decided to wait downstairs for me in the courtyard, while I went upstairs to drop off the suitcase.

When I came back and took her hand she said she felt the energy through her entire body, and she couldn't believe it.

I ran back up to my room, got my video-camera, and got her account of what she experienced on tape, and then the concierge of my hotel took a couple of photos of us together. We hung out together for at least another hour, and were amazed at the connection that we felt.

We hugged each other tightly and vowed to stay in touch, but I never heard from her again. Sometimes people are only meant to be in your life for a brief moment so that you can re-affirm each other.

She works as an on-air personality on TV, which did not surprise me one bit. She walked me back to the train station to make sure I wouldn't get lost, and promised to visit me in New York. We exchanged cards and big hugs, and held each other for the longest time. It was all very magical.

I stayed downtown, had a slice of pizza, which was nothing like New York pizza, and was right on time for the tour. We took a bus to a town called

Feosole, but my sleep disorder kicked in, and I couldn't stay awake. When that happens I don't remember a thing I saw. It's like how you forget a dream shortly after you wake up.

We walked to the San Croce Church, and then to Offizi, and the trek was exhausting. We finished at around 6 P.M. and it took forever to leave the museum. It was like a never-ending trail to follow to get out of that place.

Exhausted and hungry, I stopped for a salami and cheese sandwich, which cost 4 Euros, and a 3.50 Euro coke. Sodas in Europe are so expensive. They're more expensive than the food.

I tried on some leather jackets and to my surprise every thing I tried on fit me perfectly. I love Florence. Tomorrow will be my shopping day.

I didn't get back to my room until around 7:30. I crashed out for a while, then went out and found a locutorio, made tons of calls to friends to tell them I was in Florence, came back to my room, and transcribed the videotapes. Who even knows what I'll use them for?

The next thing I know it's midnight, and time to go to bed, so I can have a full day tomorrow.

FLORENCE, ITALY - DAY 2 - 8/26/06

I sleep until 9 A.M. again, but manage to leave the hotel by 11. I had my TV fixed, a bulb replaced, and my sink unclogged while at breakfast, and my plan is to shop all day.

I went out and bought amazing clothes. Every single store has things that fit me, except for having to shorten the sleeves a little bit. I seem to be a perfect size 48. I worry that I won't be able to close my suitcase, but I buy the clothes anyway.

One way or another I will find a way to get them home. I even bought what I thought was a winter coat.

It felt so heavy to me in the August heat of Florence, but when I got it home to New York, it felt so light and thin it was more appropriate for Spring than Winter.

I went to the train station intending to change my ticket to Rome, but I changed my mind after getting some hard to attain information. No one really speaks English, no matter what they tell you in the travel agencies back in New York.

At a street stand, I meet a beautiful blonde German girl named Sophie who had come to Florence to study fashion. She was with two guys from FIT in New York, and they all knew the clubs I hung out in on West 27th Street.

We even knew some of the same people. So that was pretty amazing. Sophie helped me pick out a couple of gifts by modeling the clothing for me, and we took a few photos together.

Me in Florence with Sophie and Friends

I had dinner in The Piazza near my hotel and came back to my room around 11:30. I had pasta for 9.80 Euros and once again a soda that cost $4.30 Euros. Soda is as expensive as oil in Europe, or at least in Italy.

I turned on the TV, watched CNN (in English), and caught some of the Jon Stewart show with my friend Matt Dillon as a guest. I packed some of my clothes and went to bed around 1 A.M.

FLORENCE, ITALY to ROME-8/27/06

I had been warned many times to look out for pickpockets on the train, and not to leave my bags for a moment on the station, lest they might be stolen. So that was on my mind when I woke up early for my last day in Florence.

I go to breakfast early, pay my hotel bill, and request to keep my room until 2 P.M., but they told me they were full, and that I had to leave by noon.

At around 11:20 I go back to the marketplace to get my new blue suede belt sized, but I can't find the guy, since the position of the stands changes every day, and I don't remember what he looked like.

I realized that the belts I like in the USA were usually at least fifty to sixty dollars, so if I could find nice belts for 15 Euros that I liked I should grab them.

I find a stand that has two nice belts I liked, and make a deal for 28 Euros for both, plus he fixed my new blue belt, and the one I was wearing.

I come back to the hotel, finish packing, and let them put my stuff in storage. I arrange for a cab to the train station and remember to request a driver who spoke English. I intended to pay him extra to help me get my stuff onto the train.

I may as well have not bothered remembering to ask for a driver who spoke English because the guy they sent spoke English about as good as I spoke Italian, which was not good at all.

He arrived right on time, just before 2 P.M., and helped me load my stuff into the car. I made my deal with him to pay him extra for helping me onto the train, so he parked, and took my luggage all the way to the "binario", which means the track where my train was supposed to be.

The only problem was that with all of my ingenious planning, I managed to outsmart myself as I often do, by arriving so early that the train was not even there yet. Needless to say, he was not able to help me on to a train that wasn't there.

I gave him a tip anyway as a thank you for his time. He found me a seat on the platform, and I read a magazine until the train came.

The train actually came around 2:30, and of course I had to drag all of my stuff on by myself.

I was supposed to be in car 11, and this time, because I was on time, I got into the right car.

I threw one bag in first, up the stairs, and then dragged my other two bags up the stairs as well, managing not to throw my back out in the process.

I put some of my things in the bin, and took my camera bag and rolling cart to my seat. Fortunately, I had some snacks and some water left.

The train was headed to Naples with a stop at Rome-Termini Station. It was a long but uneventful trip, and when we finally arrived I threw my bags off, and while setting them up on my falling luggage carrier for the umpteenth time, I meet Francesca, this smoking redhead, who hardly spoke English, but helped to guide me outside where I got openly ripped off for the first time in Europe.

I really should have known better coming from New York, because I know better than to trust anyone, but as Francesca and I emerged from the station to look for a taxi, some guy in a suit, with bad teeth and an earring approached us and asked where we were going.

Possibly trying to show off my non-existent facility for Italian, I tell him the name of my hotel, and he quotes me a price of 30 Euros for both of us. When we explain we weren't together, he tells some other guy to take her, and he starts wheeling my bags without even asking me if I wanted to go with him.

Something felt wrong, and I should have listened to my intuition, ... but I didn't. I said, "How much?" and he said "Thirty Euros." Now the hotel had told me to expect a charge of maybe 10-15 Euros so I told him it was too much.

That's when he explained to me that it was a Sunday, so there would be a surcharge, plus I had three bags, and there was a charge per bag. He didn't even have a taxi. He had a private car. As I said, I should have known much better, but I got in.

Luckily for me, on the way to the hotel, I videotaped the guy, and asked him questions on camera, which may be why he didn't victimize me any further.

I made him answer questions as part of the video documentary I was making about my trip. Without being over-dramatic, it might have even saved my life.

For a savvy New Yorker, I should have known better than to take anything but a real taxi.

Rome doesn't seem as friendly as Florence. Maybe it's just my hotel. At least the porter spoke

Spanish. The internet is out of order, and the hand towels are like dinner napkins. It's like wiping your hands on cardboard. Very satisfying!

There's no shampoo. They told me to use the bath and body gel on my hair. It doesn't seem like there's any place close to the hotel that's either fun or interesting.

However, people all over the world are very nice. I stopped into a store to ask directions on how to take the bus, and a woman gave me a bus ticket for free, and wouldn't take any money for it.

On the way home that night on the bus, I try to use my Italian, but the bus driver lets me out in a dark, and desolate section of the Via Po. Fortunately, as always happens, I find a woman who spoke no real English, but guided me to a street that I recognized.

I'm starving and so I go into a restaurant near the hotel to eat. It seemed like they were ignoring me after they sat me down at a table, and no one came over for maybe 20 minutes. I'm about to lose my temper, when a manager comes over, who was so nice to me that I let it go. He was Egyptian, but spoke Spanish, so we conversed.

I get back to my room around midnight to read the tour brochures, and ask for a wake-up call for 7:30 A.M. to start my first full day in Rome.

ROME - DAY 1 - 8/28/06

I'm at The Beverly Hills Hotel, which quite honestly is nothing like The Beverly Hills Hotel in Los Angeles that I was thinking of when I made the reservation, ... but it was fine.

I get up early to have breakfast, grab some snacks to take with me for the day, which is my little trick for staying comfortable, so I don't have to fear being hungry and having nothing to eat or drink, and it always works out well.

Most of my hotels offered a full breakfast with lots of delicious, fattening cakes, and baked goods, and I would wrap them up in napkins, and stuff them into a little bag that I carried, so that I didn't have to return to my room for most of the day.

I even had the courage to send two of my shirts to the hotel cleaners to be laundered. I would never have done that in the past, for fear that something would happen to them.

I was expecting an interesting day because it was my late father's birthday, and I know he's always watching over me.

I endure a long and difficult walk to the famed Via Veneto just to see what all the hype was about. It was only about a half an hour walk, but there were lots of obstacles along the way.

When I finally get there, I thought I was in the wrong place. This couldn't be the famed Via Veneto. I was picturing something romantic looking, with a lake, or something like that.

It was maybe five or six blocks of over-priced stores, hotels, and cafés. Nothing exciting in the least, unless you like $500. shirts.

From there I walked to the famed Spanish Steps, which I believe was named for the way the Spaniards entered the city, many years before. They took the steps because the escalator wasn't working! (Sorry, I couldn't help myself!)

I wanted to buy a leather jacket, but everything was so overpriced, and there was nothing special. Thank G-d I shopped well in Florence.

I was even toying with the idea of taking the train back to Florence to look for a leather jacket, but I had actually looked for one while I was there and didn't find anything to my liking, so I decided not to go back.

So far I'm not that impressed with Rome. I meet a Russian model named Alessa, and we have a coffee at a nearby café. She spoke English surprisingly well. We exchange numbers, and we speak again later in the evening, but we didn't get to meet up.

I wasn't willing to hassle while away on vacation. Either it's easy or it's not happening.

As I walk the streets, I meet another woman named Michelle. I had asked her directions before I noticed how beautiful she was. And she was as helpful and accommodating as she was gorgeous.

A few minutes later, two beautiful little girls ran over, ... her boyfriend's daughters, and it turns out that she was on vacation with her boyfriend, so that was that. We exchanged numbers before he came along, but he was such a nice guy that we all wound up having a nice chat.

Around 3 P.M. I make an impulsive decision to jump on a #110 sightseeing bus at the Via Veneto, and buy a 24 hour ticket, which means I can get off and on again at my desire, for 24 hours. They run constantly.

The only problem was I had another "narcolepsy" attack, and wound up sleeping through all the sights. Personally I think it's psychological, and due to stress.

I get off at Termini Station, the main terminal, and take bus #92 back to my hotel where I shower, change, and relax, then take the #63 bus back down to the Via Veneto area to have dinner.

I wind up at an outdoor restaurant sitting next to an interesting couple from England. She was half Indian, with one of those interesting, exotic kind of faces that could either be gorgeous, or hideous, depending on the angle. I always found that fascinating.

The talk turned to my writing for the famed Friars Roasts, and we had a spirited conversation. They were really fun and we exchanged information before bidding each other "adieu."

I brought the rest of my meal home with me, and turned in around midnight after trying to watch some TV. I happened to get Legally Blonde, but couldn't watch it all the way through because Reese Witherspoon's character was just so obnoxious, I couldn't take it. I guess that makes her a good actress!

Tomorrow is set to be a sightseeing day, and I'm planning on going inside The Colosseum. That's something I always wanted to do because I'm fascinated by ancient history.

I'm actually looking forward to going home on Thursday.

ROME - DAY 2 - 8/29/06

I get up at 7:30 A.M. and get to the dining room about 9 A.M. It takes me a long time to get ready in the morning. I want to get to the Colosseum as early as possible, because the day has a way of getting away from me, especially when you have ADHD.

So I get on the #3 trolley on Viale Regina Margherita which is only two blocks from the hotel. The concierge at my hotel tells me I'll recognize The Colosseum when I see it, and that's how I'd know when to get off.

I did tell the bus driver in Italian where I was going, but as usual they make very little effort to communicate, or even tell you if they understood what you said.

A maniac got on the bus and sat facing me. I noticed him waiting to board, because he was dressed nicely in a suit, but had long, dark, greasy black hair worn flat back, and down to his shoulders.

He was carrying a nice leather briefcase, and I remember thinking, "I wonder if that's considered a hip hairstyle in Italy for a well dressed, successful guy."

That thought evaporated kind of quickly as soon as he boarded, and sat in his seat side-saddle, which I thought he was doing to be polite, to give the other riders more room, until he started literally growling like an animal, and bearing his teeth.

It was both frightening and amusing to watch him, as he seemed to alternate between different personalities. He spoke out loud in a Devil's kind of voice in Italian, like a low beast-like growl, making elaborate hand gestures, and occasionally switching to a softer voice like a girl. Once I even thought I heard some English.

As people realized he was insane they moved away from him giving him a wide berth. He seemed dangerous, and I wondered what he had in that beautiful leather briefcase. Probably tools for carving people up.

I wanted to avoid his eyes, but I couldn't keep from looking at him. I was drawn to witness his insanity and he didn't stop growling and grimacing for a moment, as if he was possessed.

I get up to ask the bus driver a question, and someone takes my seat. I return and take the only other seat which leaves me literally sitting face to face with him across an aisle.

I realized I had to make a video recording of this nut, so I maneuvered my video camera out of my bag, and turned it on him without him seeing. It was a hard thing to do, and probably dangerous if he had caught me, so I had to keep looking away and just hope I still had him in frame.

I filmed him for about six minutes until we reached The Colosseum.

I had the feeling that he was going to follow me off the bus since he had been staring at me a lot, but fortunately he didn't. There are some very sick people wandering around this world, and you just have to hope you never come face to face with them.

I don't think I'll ever forget the shock of seeing him growling out loud, and baring his teeth like a wild animal.

Outside the Colosseum, I meet Cassandra, a tall thin beauty who was not only repping a tour, but was also promoting a "club-crawl" later that night. Once you've done the club scene in New York, nothing quite compares, especially when your "posse" is made up of tourists from all over the world, who have never met each other before, and need twenty beers or so to loosen up.

The regular line for The Colosseum was so long, it took at least an hour to gain entrance, so I made the smart move of buying a tour for 20 Euros, which included a second tour later on of The Forum and Palatine Area.

It was very hot, and there was lots of climbing making our way around The Colosseum, but it was fascinating, especially seeing the narrow corridors where they kept the slaves and the lions, and how they raised the lions into the ring from down below on lifts. I was glad I had packed some snacks and water.

I got lots of photos and around 4:30 P.M. I make my way back to the hotel, making sure to get lost on the way because I was so tired and hot, and getting lost was the perfect addition.

I took the #3 bus instead of the #3 trolley. Of course the bus broke down and we all had to get off and wait for another one. It's at those moments when you're hungry, thirsty, sweaty, and alone in another country, when you ask yourself why you're even there in the first place, and not at home in your comfortable apartment enjoying the air conditioning and a nice, cold drink.

Finally another bus came along but I wasn't sure it was the right one. Once again no bus driver has ever actually responded to my request, and this driver was no exception when I asked "Puo dirmi quando schendere?" Can you tell me when to get off? They all give me the equivalent of a three act play in Italian as an answer, and I just nod my head as if I understand, and pay my fare.

So I didn't know what stop to get off, and they neglected to tell me. I took a guess, which was foolish knowing my non-existent sense of direction, and wound up miles away from where I needed to go.

I got off at the second Regina Margherita stop and I needed Via Salaria, which I only learned after the fact.

It's always nice to be stranded, and lost, but even more-so when you're hot and uncomfortable. As I walked along, I went into a phone store and used both Spanish and English to buy a new SIM card, and a great phone card to call the States.

I walk for what seems like a very long time, and finally get back to my room at 5:30 P.M. and immediately fall asleep for a couple of hours. I go out for dinner at around 10:30, once again not realizing that this is not New York where you can find restaurants open at any hour.

I pass up a nearby Chinese restaurant, because who goes to Italy for Chinese food? (That question does not require an answer!)

ROME - DAY 3 - 8/30/06

I wake up early to go to The Vatican. The concierge tells me to take trolley #19 to the last stop.

During the course of the day, I meet three amazing women, all of whom I feel I connected with on a deep level. I exchange numbers with all of them, since they all said they were planning on coming to New York.

Since I am writing this long after, I can tell you that I never heard from any of them, but that's okay. It's just nice while it's happening.

The first one I meet while on my way to the trolley. Her name was Miriam, and she was so cute and bubbly, mostly because she had learned English by dubbing American films. She had a cute little tattoo on her right ankle.

Then I get on trolley #19, and luckily meet a Rumanian woman named Irina, (who was not one of the three mentioned above), and it's a good thing I did. When I told her I was going to The Vatican, and was told to get off at the last stop, she told me that was totally wrong.

As luck would have it she worked at The Vatican, and was going there also, so she was kind enough to actually take me. This was akin to a miracle. What are the odds?

And to tell you the truth those are also the kind of things that happen to me more often that you would expect. A lot of ridiculous things happen to me, but also a lot of nice things.

It's like my Higher Power is always watching over me. Someone always seems to offer to take me someplace so I don't get lost. It happened to me in Japan many times.

This lady had me get off the trolley at the next to last stop, and take the metro with her for one stop to Cipro, the stop for The Vatican Museum, which is where I wound up going.

Some people are just so wonderful, and they pass through your life just when they need to be there. True angels!

I had heard that you had to wait for hours to get into The Vatican, and I was in no mood for that, but the line for the Vatican Museum was moving quickly, so I jumped on that, and 12 Euros later, I was inside.

It's funny, but when you're traveling alone and you only have to pay for yourself, things are much more reasonable. Once you're paying for some-one else, you double the cost, and you really start to feel it.

Anyway, the Vatican Museum is HUGE. I wanted to just get a taste of it, and then see The Sistine Chapel, but you can't do it that way. Once you start you're locked in.

I started climbing up staircases, and walked through literally fifty rooms, each one with a sign and an arrow that pointed to the Sistine Chapel, only it was never there.

After a while, it felt like a joke. It's kind of like seeing a road sign in New York that reads, "Buffalo 400 miles". You know it's somewhere ahead, but who knows where.

Personally, I was just as impressed with The Hall of Maps in terms of beauty, as I was with the ceiling of The Sistine Chapel. But that's just me.

Finally, after hall #55, I was almost running to get to the end and actually see The Sistine Chapel. It's the very last thing you see.

By the time you get there, you've already seen such incredible things, you're almost numb to the beauty and artistry of it.

No photos are allowed, so it was very hard for me to get one! (LOL) They have guards all over. I did it with no flash, just because I didn't know if I'd ever be back again, and if my grandchildren ever needed to know what the ceiling of the Sistine Chapel looked like, at least I'd have a photo somewhere.

Leaving the museum is just as difficult as getting there. It winds down forever, and just when you think there absolutely can not be another floor, there is.

I eat in the cafeteria, which had good food and was very reasonable. A salami and cheese sandwich was only 2.60 Euros, and a good size Coke was only 1.50 Euros.

There's no ice, but they do have mustard, which no other place seemed to have. They gave it out like it was gold, ... one pack at a time.

I finally make my way to the street, and back to the Cipro Metro stop to take the train back to Termini, in order to catch the Archeobus, which was the tour bus, so that I could see The Appian Way.

It's an easy trip to Termini, and when I come out I manage to find the bus area. It's a huge station and I only have ten minutes to catch the last bus of the day. What else is new? (LOL)

You can't buy your tickets on the bus at that stop, only during the course of the trip, so the bus driver sends me over to find a booth. On my way, I see the most amazing woman.

We catch each other's eye, but there is no time to talk, and I make my choice to buy my ticket and catch the bus. Imagine my surprise when I get to my bus and see that she is my tour guide.

I wind up sitting right next to her across the aisle, and we talk the whole way. She tells me that her name is Marcia, and that she is an actress, and when I tell her that I did some producing, she says, "I had heard you were a comedy writer."

She never told me who told her that, and it drove me crazy for the whole trip. I don't know why I didn't just ask her! To this day I don't know.

She had great teeth and an amazing smile, but she stayed on her cell phone too long and spoke too loudly.

At one point, I ask her a question about a particular aqueduct, and she calls a female colleague of hers, and hands me her cell phone so her friend could explain it to me.

When I give her back her phone she says her friend told her to get my address because they're coming to New York to visit me. Guess what? Never happened!

It was my last night in Rome, and it would have been perfect to spend it with her, but The Universe had other plans for me, and she had plans with some friends.

It was actually the best thing that could have happened, because I still had to pack and wake up about 6:30 A.M. for an early cab to the airport.

I had almost forgotten about this but during that bus trip a very strange Indian woman wearing a very bizarre hat, requested to sit next to me even though the seat had many items stored under it.

It was so important to her to sit there that she just sat on top of those things. She asked a million questions interrupting my conversation with Marcia, and opened a very large map that went across my face. She never even said, "Excuse me."

So as the tour bus pulled back into Termini Station, and before I said my final goodbye to Marcia, I read her chakras, did a color reading on her and examined her hand to read her energy right there in the street.

She was in so much awe of what I was telling her that she couldn't stop hugging me, but then she began to feel awkward and stopped.

Her friends were watching and didn't understand what was going on. All of a sudden she's hugging this guy from the bus!

She was determined to have me try the food in a certain restaurant that she liked, and was laboring over describing to me how to get there, but when she left, I jumped on the 92 bus back to Via Po, to go back to my hotel and pack.

When I get off the bus, I see this clothing outlet still open with men's clothes, and a sale sign.

I walk in and the next thing I know I had met the third fantastic woman of the day. Carolina was so amazing, tan and tattooed, ... and married unfortunately for me, but she took so much time with me, and sold me a great jacket.

And I practiced my Italian, and mixed it with Spanish and I stayed with her for about an hour. We also took photos, exchanged Healing energy, and made plans to see each other some time in the future.

We exchanged information, and of course we never spoke again, but it was wonderful, and neither of us wanted to part. She just kept hugging me, and in a different time, or a different place, who knows what would have happened.

I think we have many soul mates out there. The only problem is that most of them seem to be married! (LOL)

It was 8:30 P.M. and it was time to go back and start packing. I was going home tomorrow. Yayyyyyyyyyyyyyy!

LAST DAY IN ROME & HOME TO NYC-8/31/06

I had a wake-up call for 6:30 A.M. It's such a good thing that none of those girls I met was free last night, because I needed every moment I had to pack. After I got out of the shower, I had to figure out how to pack all of the clothes I had bought in Florence, so I could manage my luggage and get on the plane.

I go in for breakfast by 7:30 and am done by about 8. I had already emptied my room safe and packed my jacket pockets the night before as I always do, to prevent me from forgetting everything due to my fear of traveling, and the confusion caused by my ADHD.

I take my snacks for the plane and fill my water bottle forgetting completely that they would probably take it away from me at the airport. I go to pay my bill, and they try to just tell me the amount without presenting me with the itemized bill.

The guy says "560 Euros please". I say, "May I review the bill please?" He looks at me as if no one had ever asked to examine the bill before, then says "Oh yes, here it is."

The bill is always correct. They just don't see the need to show it to you.

There was one, nasty, evil concierge, and he was the only one on duty when I had to arrange for my car to take me to the airport at 9 A.M. He tries to tell me to leave later than I wanted to, but I'd always rather sit an extra hour in the airport than be late, or running to catch my plane.

I have the bellman come up at 8:40 for my bags, and he seems pleasantly surprised at the 2 Euro tip I give him. Nobody tips in Europe. Speaking of tipping, I was glad to see that my luggage cart tipped over for him too, so it wasn't only my fumbling that did that. Something is always wrong with my luggage.

I started carrying my camera bag and only rolled my garment bag, and my regular suitcase, which made it a lot easier, but my garment bag still got caught on everything I passed, including couches, people, seats, and especially metal stanchions, which seemed to be set up in front of every escalator so that my luggage wouldn't fit between them.

I even accidentally banged into two Carabiniere, (Italian policemen) while I was on my way through the airport.

The driver was right on time, and had a nice Mercedes wagon. It was nice and roomy, and he got me to Fiumicino Airport by 9:30 A.M. I was actually the first passenger to check in for my flight.

They weren't even planning on checking anyone in until 10 A.M., even though they ask you to arrive three hours before. My bag was so heavy they charged me another 20 Euros, but it didn't even bother me. For some reason their money doesn't seem real.

The trip to the airport only cost me 50 Euros which was a lot better than paying 30 Euros to that crook I encountered when I arrived for a much shorter trip.

So I'm all checked in by 10:30 A.M. and I take a nice Sky Train to my gate. I was doing okay with my ADHD except that I confused my seat row with the gate number, so I went looking for Gate 21, instead of Gate 26.

Fortunately they were not far from each other, which was a blessing, and a big karmic change.

In the past, if I had made such a mistake, it would have been more likely that I would have needed to get to some far-off gate like Gate 46, where I would be racing across the entire airport to get there before I missed my flight.

So that was a nice change. I was still wrong but at least I wasn't too far off.

Now it's 11 A.M., and I'm already at Gate 26, eating my snacks and drinking my water, and writing notes about my trip so I wouldn't forget anything.

I want to change my money back into dollars but at the airport they charge you 6 Euros plus 6%, so 100 Euros would give me back only $94. I decide to wait until I get back to my own bank at home.

As I've said before, just once I'd like to travel without hearing someone yell out, "Excuse me sir, does this belong to you?" And of course it happened again.

This time, it wasn't my passport and money, it was just my itinerary, but it had phone numbers, and personal information on it, so it's nice, and lucky for me that so many people are kind and honest, ... for the most part.

For some reason they let me board early with first class and Zone 1 even though I was in Zone 9. I didn't hear what they said, and they didn't make me go back. Maybe they sensed how badly I wanted to get home.

Once through the gate, our bags were checked once more, but just perfunctorily. They did however take my water, and made me take off my shoes.

They almost didn't allow both of my bags on the plane but then they relented. At that point, I was so exhausted, I didn't even argue. Whatever they wanted would have been okay.

I'm in an aisle seat, 21F, with lots of room, and I'm right near the bathroom. It's all good so far.

I thank my Higher Power once again for allowing me the strength to make this trip, and just settle back into my seat waiting excitedly to be back in New York City, where I belong.

Epilogue - Just to show the extent of my confusion and how two weeks away in Europe "discombobulated" me, the morning after I arrived home and woke up, I put toilet paper down over my own toilet seat before I used it.

CHAPTER

5

My Widowmaker Heart Attack

Fear of illness is a very common fear, and rightly so. If you don't have your health you have nothing. It's been proven to me several times already. I'm a believer.

On the list of scary things, close to the top must be having a heart attack. Just the thought that your heart stopped working is pretty anxiety inducing.

Mine came out of nowhere. I had never been sick a day in my life. At least with nothing serious.

It was December 17th, 2015. I'll never forget the day. It was pouring rain and I had an appointment with a new chiropractor. Actually he wasn't new in practice but he was new to me. My appointment was at 2:30.

Around 1 P.M. I started feeling this uncomfortable feeling in my chest. On the left side. Nothing too severe but kind of like a cramp. I rubbed it and it felt better. So I told myself it's probably just muscular because to my knowledge you can't rub away a heart attack.

I had been doing a lot of pushups lately and I thought that maybe I was just getting some muscle soreness. But it didn't go away.

I was tempted to cancel my chiropractor's appointment because I really don't like going out in the pouring rain. I remember having the thought that maybe I should just get back into bed. Luckily I didn't do that because a lot of people do and they never get out of bed.

That was my first stroke of luck that day, making that decision.

So I left the house around 1:30 and got on the subway and the pain was getting a bit more intense so I just kept rubbing, and that seemed to help. But it just helped for a few minutes, and then it came back.

I got off the subway at my stop, walked up about two flights of stairs, and made my way to the street. I had about six blocks to walk down busy 7th Avenue in Manhattan, and for some unknown reason I decided to turn down 50th Street even though I was going to 46th Street.

I have no idea why but I did. By that point the pain was getting pretty intense and I thought I should probably tell someone, which is a pretty awkward thing to do.

Especially for me, who can be very shy in those kinds of circumstances. Not like I had a lot of experience with anything like that, but it's very awkward to stop someone and tell them you think you're having a heart attack, ... because what if you're not?

But then I thought with my medical background I'd be an awful moron if I didn't tell anyone and just died in the street. With that I notice a police van stopped at a red light in the middle of the block, with four cops in the van.

I knock on the window and say to the cop nearest to me in a very calm voice, "I'm sorry to bother you, but I think I'm having a heart attack." And he says to me, "Well I think you should go to the hospital." To which I say, "Well that's why I'm telling you. I'm not just telling everybody!" To which he says, "Well we're stuck in traffic it'll probably be faster if you walk." To which I respond, "Well, where is the nearest hospital?" And he didn't know.

Now to tell you the truth I had expected them to pull me into the van, put on the siren and race me to a hospital. That's not what happened at all.

None of the four cops knew where there was a hospital in the middle of Manhattan. So the cop that was driving looked on his phone and I guess he was looking for hospitals.

He says to me, "Do you have Google maps?" Now you have to picture this, ... I'm standing in the pouring rain, holding an umbrella, probably in the midst of having a heart attack and he wants to know if I have Google maps.

I say "No" and he says, "Well you should probably download Google Maps", and that's when I walked away. The whole thing started feeling stupid to me. Like a scene from a Woody Allen movie. I tell the cops I'm having a heart attack and their advice is to download Google Maps so I can find my way to a hospital by foot.

I recall having told them I was on my way to a chiropractor's appointment and as I walked away one cop yells out, "Do you want us to call you an ambulance?", and the way things were going I thought if I said "Yes" he'd say, "Ok, you're an ambulance!" Like that old kid's joke.

So I just say "No thanks. I'll try and get to the chiropractor and maybe he can help me." But I could only get another half a block because the pain was getting very intense.

Now I'm right across the street from Radio City Music Hall and the Tonight Show with Jimmy Fallon, and there was another cop directing traffic. I say the same thing to him, "I'm sorry to bother you but I think I'm having a heart attack."

He was on a walkie talkie and says to me, "Stand over there" and motions for me to stand on the side behind a metal stanchion.

I wait a few minutes and say to him, "Are they coming?" And HE says, "Oh sorry I didn't call them yet!" No one seemed particularly upset that I might be having a heart attack. In retrospect I wonder if it was because I was so calm.

A few minutes later a fire engine comes roaring up on the other side of the street from where I was standing and I walk over.

About 4 or 5 firemen got off the truck and one of them says to me, "Who's the patient?" And I say "Me!" so another of them says, "Well then climb up on the truck." And I say "Really?" and he laughs and says, "Naah, we're just f*@king with you!" They all thought that was funny.

At that moment a real ambulance pulls up and two guys get out who think it's hilarious that both their names are Mike. They're like, "Hi, I'm Mike and this is Mike!"

They take me in the ambulance take off my shirt, start an I.V. and begin to ask me what felt like a long, involved medical history. I ask them if they could do that on the way to the hospital, and they say "No."

I identify myself as a doctor and tell them I'm pretty sure they could ask me the same questions while we were driving but they wouldn't give in. They were stubborn and I was in no mood or position to argue.

You don't want to fight with the guys who supposedly are trying to save you. As I recall some of the questions sounded as dumb as "Did you ever have an uncle that felt nauseous?"

Finally they decide they have enough information to start driving me to the hospital but they want to take me to a hospital where I don't have a personal doctor on staff. I plead with them to take me to a hospital where my doctor has privileges and they finally do.

They don't turn on the siren either and when I ask them why they say I don't fall within the parameters of using a siren. I was like, "How seriously do you have to be sick or hurt before you use a siren? I hear them all the time."

The answer was that they were not convinced I was having a heart attack, ... as if it was up to them to decide, ... and it turned out that the kind of heart attack I had did not show up on an EKG.

They also try to convince me that it was safer for me NOT to use the siren because then they would have to speed through red lights, and because it was raining, and the streets were slick, they felt it was safer not to speed.

So they drove very slowly and carefully and stopped at all the lights. I'm lying there with an I.V. in my arm and luckily I had the presence of mind to call one of my daughters to tell her where I was going, and also called my primary care physician to let him know I was being taken in.

And it's a good thing I did because cell phones did not work in the Emergency Room, which is a very foolish circumstance. That's exactly when they should be working so that you could call your family or someone important.

Anyway while we're driving I feel something wet squirt onto my cheek. I ask what it was and they tell me "Nitroglycerine!" I say, "It's supposed to go under your tongue not on your face" and unbelievably they say, "Don't worry, that's close enough." I knew better but again was in no position to argue.

While they drove slowly and stopped for all the lights the pain in my chest was increasing. When we finally got to the hospital, which felt like a very long time due to the traffic, they wheel me out into the pouring rain and the emergency room doors that are supposed to open automatically for a stretcher would not open. Seriously! They would not open.

And the ambulance attendant was wheeling me back and forth to try and get the doors to open. I felt like a credit card being swiped in a slot.

Finally he had to climb up on the door and open it manually while saying, "Don't worry we'll get you in there."

They wheeled me in and then had to lift me up to transfer me from their stretcher to a hospital gurney, and there I laid in the emergency room for the next nine hours, from 3 P.M. until midnight.

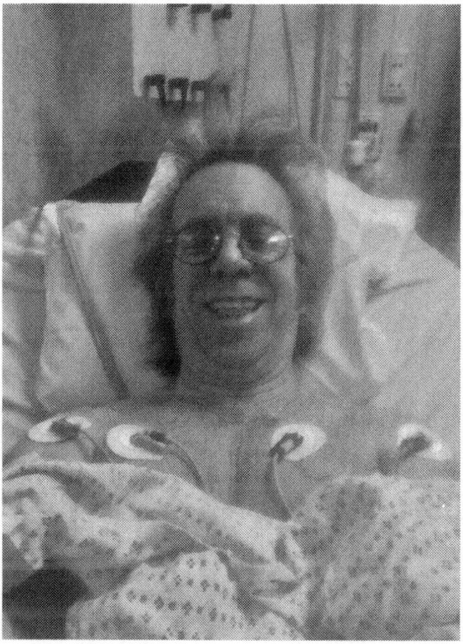

Managing to smile even during a heart attack! Always try and stay positive!

Luckily for me the emergency room doctor who examined me put me on a blood thinner right away and that's probably what saved my life. It wasn't until the next day that I found out I had had a dreaded "widowmaker" heart attack, and was approximately 95% blocked in the major artery to my heart.

At one point they wheeled me into a back corner of the emergency room near a wall to make room for patients just coming in and a nurse came over and gave me some kind of set up where she said, "If you need a nurse just press this button."

Over the next few hours I pressed and pressed and no one ever came. I had to yell out from my bed to employees passing by to please get me a nurse.

I found that I had to advocate for myself quite often, which at first feels awkward for me to do, but I have to challenge those feelings as not being accurate or valid, and go against my uncomfortability to ask for help, because when you're all alone, if you don't advocate for yourself, no one else can or will.

They couldn't find a bed in the cardiac unit for me until midnight. At 10:30 they told me they found a room for me and I told my oldest daughter that she could leave to go home to her kids.

My other daughter had been there earlier. It took from 10:30 until midnight for them to find someone who could wheel me to my room.

They call it "Transport" and I guess it's a very technical thing that requires a great degree of skill because they weren't able to find anyone who could do it for 90 whole minutes.

Once again I had to yell out to passing employees to ask if they could please wheel me to my room. I was really glad to see that I could advocate for myself when I needed to. It got easier as the time went on.

Finally at midnight I got my room in the cardiac unit and that's when I started receiving what I would consider to be proper care. But I still did not see a cardiologist. That was not to happen until the next morning.

Before I drifted off to sleep a nice medical assistant wearing a yamulke came to my bedside and told me that things looked more serious than they thought. He said there was a chemical in my bloodstream called Troponin which is not supposed to be there. If it's there at all it's supposed to be like 0.002 whatevers. It only appears if you have a heart attack.

When I came in mine registered at 11, then went to 18, and by midnight was 24. He said that in the morning they would probably have to do an angioplasty on me with a little balloon on it because I probably had some kind of a blockage.

I kept asking if I could see a cardiologist but there was no one there at midnight. He said that in the morning there was a doctor whose specialty was going into your heart through a blood vessel in your arm instead of the groin, and that sounded good to me. Or as good as something like that could sound under the circumstances.

Then before he left he said, “but if you feel bad pain during the night call us and we’ll do it as an emergency.” That didn’t sound that great to me, because who knows who’s on call during the night?

I was afraid I might get someone without a lot of experience and it certainly wouldn’t be the guy who goes through your arm. I didn’t want just anybody fooling around in my groin, much less my heart!

So with all those thoughts swimming around in my head I had to try and go to sleep. Not an easy task!

During the night, I awoke and had some pain, but the thought of going into surgery as an emergency was a bit overwhelming to me, so because I believe in the power of prayer, I said a little prayer and went back to sleep. I made it through the night.

In the morning they woke me up around 6 to start taking blood, which they did constantly, but I didn’t get to see a real cardiologist until around 9:30. I had already called my primary care physician again and asked if he could intervene in some way to get a cardiologist to come and examine me.

Within a few minutes a nice female cardiologist came to see me and declared, "Yes, this looks a lot more serious than we thought. I'm going to get you into the operating room as soon as possible."

And then she disappeared and I didn't see her again until much later.

But before she did, I told her I'd like to meet the surgeon before he puts me under, and she agreed, but the surgeon didn't come to my room.

They finally came for me around 10:30 or 11 A.M. as I recall, and started me on some kind of light anesthetic, because you're basically awake while they do this procedure, and they started wheeling me to the operating room.

For whatever reason I don't remember feeling nervous. It was probably the anesthetic.

But I kept asking to meet the surgeon. Just before they wheeled me through the doors of the O.R. a nice young guy with long hair like mine popped out of a doorway and introduced himself as the surgeon. His name was Dr. Babak (Bobby) Hassid.

I recall him saying to me, "My specialty is going in through your arm. It's my duty to tell you that your arm could go permanently numb, but in all my years of doing this it's never happened even once." I said to him, "I trust you. Just do what you have to do."

The next thing I remember is that I'm naked face up on the operating table and they're shaving my groin area just in case the arm thing doesn't work, and they have to go in that way. On a personal note, I liked the way it looked so much I've been shaving it that way ever since! (LOL) TMI?

So I'm on the operating table and they strap down my arm, and I'm looking away to the other side of the room, and I see my heart on a TV screen. I can actually see them threading something through my blood vessel and I'm feeling this back and forth sawing motion, and it started feeling quite uncomfortable, but because I'm always joking around, ... even in a situation like that, ... I remember saying to the surgeon, "I feel you in my heart. Not in a romantic way, but I feel you in there."

And he said, "Ok, I'll give you more anesthetic", and that's the last thing I remember until I woke up in my room. He put in one stent and opened the blocked artery, which was the main artery to the left side of the heart, the left anterior descending (LAD) artery.

Around 5 P.M. that day he came to my room to visit me, and he hugged me and told me that I was a miracle. I told him that HE was the miracle because he went into my heart through my arm and saved me.

The way I look at it with the whole weird police thing, and ambulance and emergency room fiasco, was that through no fault of their own, they accidentally saved my life.

Since that time I take five medications every day, and I go for 6 month check-ups in which they do a cardiogram. One of the last times I went they told me I was doing fine but I requested them to check something else and they wound up doing an echo cardiogram and came back with the news that I had a torn mitral valve, and might need to have it fixed surgically.

Unfortunately there's no conservative way of doing that yet. I was hoping that Dr. Hassid could go back in through my arm, but he doesn't do that.

I went to Columbia Presbyterian and had a consultation with one of the top heart surgeons in the world who had operated on Bill Clinton and Barbara Walters, and also happened to have operated on my parents.

It seems that the conservative approach has not been approved yet for people as "young and healthy" as I am, so they said I could wait. The conservative procedure called the Mitra Clip for repairing the mitral valve, was invented by Dr. Oz from TV, who I had met before at The Friars Club and also at Joan Rivers' funeral, but I didn't know if he'd remember me.

As I left the surgeon's office in the hospital, and was walking down a long corridor, I passed a group of doctors who were being lectured to by someone, but I couldn't see who it was.

Suddenly an arm reached out and grabbed me from out of nowhere, and a voice said "Jeffrey, I know why you're here and let me tell you about the Mitra Clip" and it was Dr. Oz himself. Once again, ... that can't even happen. What are the odds? We even took pictures together right there in the hospital corridor.

With the amazing Dr. Oz

They said they've seen people in my condition go years before they need surgery, and thank G-d I was not showing any symptoms, so I go every six months and on my most recent check-up they told me that my heart was looking better than it did six months before. Another true miracle. And that's after recovering from Covid 19 double pneumonia!

In the meantime in the next chapter you'll read my most recent attempt at confronting fear and the confusion I face from my ADHD by traveling to Japan all alone. Alone as in "all by myself!" (LOL)

CHAPTER

6

Attacking Japan

In my quest to challenge my uncomfortability and do all the things that other people seem to do quite easily, I decided to tackle a solo trip to Japan, a mere 14 hour flight away from New York City.

I'm not sure why, but I always had kind of a fascination with Japan. I love Japanese people and the culture and it's hard for me to grasp that we were at war with them only 75 years ago trying to destroy each other.

So I joined the Japan society and started studying Japanese. I have a good friend who's married to a Japanese woman and two years in a row he was supposed to go with me to Japan and both times he had to cancel after I was really psyched to go.

The second time his wife had suggested that he and I go alone because it would be much more fun for us. After that disappointing cancellation I realized I might never get there if I didn't go alone.

And everyone in my Japanese class told me it's a great place to go alone because the people are friendly and "everyone speaks English."

I came to find out how untrue that last part was. It's true that everyone was very friendly but hardly anyone outside of the concierges at the hotels spoke conversational English. More on that later.

I decided I'd go in October because the weather is still nice there then and I had just finished level 1 Japanese for the third time. I had taken it a few years before when I was dating a Japanese girl and wanted to be able to speak to her in Japanese.

That relationship didn't last long enough for me to learn much and I wound up taking it twice more expecting to be traveling with my friend.

So I went out to research travel agencies who were familiar with Japan. I reached out to a Japanese friend and she turned me on to a Japanese agency that helped me plan my trip.

I did the whole thing as if I was in a trance, like an out of body experience, not really thinking that on October 2, 2019 I would actually be on a plane to Japan. It took a TREMENDOUS amount of planning, especially because Tokyo has so many districts and I wasn't sure where I wanted to stay.

I had to research all of them, choose hotels, find out about purchasing a Japan Rail Pass which you can only purchase outside of Japan, find a reliable Wifi rental place because as hi-tech as Japan is they don't have a strong wifi signal all over, so you have to rent one and pick it up when you land, and tons more details that had to be figured out, decided on and taken care of. All in advance of going!

It's very easy to become overwhelmed with details when you have ADHD.

I decided on a 14 day stay because you have to take off a day on either end for traveling and I couldn't see staying less time for such a long trip. As you read previously I had flown to Europe but that was only 6-7 hours. This was 14 hours in the air.

I decided to spend a week in Tokyo, then take a shinkansen (bullet train) to Kyoto for three days, do a day trip to Osaka, and then take a bullet train back to Tokyo for another two days before flying home.

You can't fly back to the U.S. from Kyoto, and I didn't want to stress myself out by taking the bullet train and having to run right to the airport to fly home.

I try and plan things in a way to make myself comfortable. It's an important lesson I have learned.

October 2nd finally comes and it feels like a dream. Except it's real.

My car picks me up at 8:15 A.M. for an 11:30 A.M. JAL flight to Narita Airport. That's another choice to make, whether to land in either Narita or Haneda Airport. Neither of them are particularly close to Tokyo and a taxi from Narita would run around $250.00, but I was told it was better to fly into Narita.

Fortunately there was a shuttle bus that ran from the airport and that stopped at all the hotels. I was staying in Shinjuku at the Hilton Hotel, which happened to be one of the stops.

As usual, I traveled with three bags, a garment bag, a large suitcase and a leather carry on bag in which I kept my video camera, my selfie stick, battery chargers, and other personal and useful items.

My TSA pre-check helps me get through security fairly quickly and I make my way to the gate to await boarding. I had a couple of hours to wait but that never bothers me.

I'd always rather be early than late because time is a strange concept for someone with ADHD and it's very easy to be late, which adds tremendous stress to whatever it is that you're doing. At least it does for me.

I had decided to try traveling premium economy going to Japan, which was much more expensive, but I got to wait in a special lounge that served snacks.

I start taking photos of everything around me because I like to document my travels. Mostly because I can't believe I'm really doing it.

We wind up boarding around noon instead of 11:30 A.M. and I have a seat on the aisle kind of close to the front where business class starts. Right away things start going awry. One of the supposed advantages of Premium Economy was that your seat was supposed to recline. Mine was not working well.

On top of that I bought Wifi for $20. hoping to watch some Netflix specials and that didn't work either. The flight attendants gave me forms to fill out seeking some kind of reimbursement but JAL makes it almost impossible to get in touch with them and when I finally did they denied that I had any problems at all, and denied my claims.

Around 4 P.M. after only four hours in the air, the plane went dark. They turned out all the lights and closed the window shades as if it was night-time. I asked the flight attendant why and she said because it was 5 A.M. in Japan, and didn't explain any further.

I guess they were preparing the 250 Japanese people on board for their return home. I didn't see any non-Japanese person besides myself so basically the whole plane fell asleep except for me. I roamed the aisle to keep the blood in my legs from clotting!

People had warned me to buy compression socks, which I did, but I'm still not sure of the difference between compression socks and just very tight socks! (LOL)

The rest of the trip was kind of like a dream state. I don't really remember it and possibly I drifted in and out of sleep. The way you don't recall a dream that's how I feel about the flight. It just seemed like it would never end.

My plan was to get to Japan while it was still light out. The thought of getting somewhere at night, in a strange land where I don't know anyone, or the language is very upsetting to me. (Fear!) We landed at Narita airport right on time around 2:40 P.M.

The airport is HUGE, and no one on my plane knew what carousel our luggage would be on in baggage claim. I made my way around, finally found it, got my bag and made it through customs pretty easily.

The Customs agent just wanted to know why I was there and I told him it had always been my dream to see Japan. He seemed to like that!

The hard part was finding the JR office to get my Japan Rail Pass in order to get my voucher activated for 7 days. Fortunately I found an empty luggage cart so I didn't have to lug my luggage around. (Just noticed the connection between "lug" and "luggage" as I was writing this. They have to be connected in some way! LOL)

I finally found the JR office and had to wait on a long line to get my pass. You need the pass in order to ride the bullet trains. I didn't want to go to my hotel and then have to come back to the airport to get it so although I was so tired, I decided to get it done right then and there.

Next I had to find the post office on the third level of the airport in order to get my portable wifi.

I had fears of not knowing how to use it and not being able to ask anyone to help me, or not understanding what they were telling me, but fortunately my fears were unfounded.

The people were very helpful and I knew enough Japanese to get it to work, which was amazing. Then I had to go back downstairs and find the limousine bus counter to get a bus that went to my hotel.

I needed a round trip ticket to Tokyo and back. It wasn't that easy for me to make myself understood.

People really didn't speak much English but we eventually managed to understand each other. Then I went to the limo bus area to wait for my bus, which was #16, and which I thought was a good sign as it's one of my lucky numbers. It finally came in and just 2 hours and 40 minutes later I was dropped off at my hotel.

It was the Tokyo Hilton and it was gorgeous and smelled fantastic as soon as you entered the lobby. Plus I was greeted enthusiastically by the staff, who were grouped in the lobby like a welcoming committee. It was almost as if they already knew me and were awaiting my arrival.

My room was absolutely beautiful. It was a suite with Japanese styling and I liked it right away. I had a friend named Kaori who is a comedian who used to live in New York and now moved back to Japan, and I called her right away.

She came over to meet me at 7:30. Security is very tight so I had to go to the lobby to meet her and bring her up to my room. She was amazed at how big it was, because most rooms in Japan are very small.

She looked amazing, with pink hair, and because she's also a comedian she came prepared with a sense of humor that allowed us to take Instagram photos in the shower, acting as if she was one of the amenities that came with the room.

With Kaori in the shower!

She took me out touring, and we hung out till about midnight. It was a wonderful first night, and a great start to the whole trip.

TOKYO - DAY 2

For some reason I woke up at 4:30 A.M. and stayed up. I was able to sign up for an all day tour that started at 8:10 A.M. so it was lucky I didn't sleep in. We went all over including a boat ride, and an authentic Japanese lunch, (as if I would know the difference if it wasn't authentic! LOL)

I made a very unlikely friend. It was a man from Australia named Tudor who on the surface was very unlike me. But to show you how unimportant those superficial things really are, he was such a nice guy and we got along so well that he actually came to see me perform in a comedy show the next night.

With my buddy Tudor in Japan. He took care of me and made sure I didn't get lost!

We did the whole tour together and he helped me find my way back to the bus each time when I was sure I'd get lost and that they'd all leave without me, leaving me lost in Japan.

Those are always how my fears go. I'll be lost and left alone. I have no idea where that came from but it's there on a daily basis.

I was so exhausted by the time we got back from all the walking and the fear that went with it that I conked out around 8:30 and slept till the morning.

TOKYO - DAY 3

I had always heard that the Japanese subway system was the most difficult in the world, and because of my difficulty in traveling just the thought of having to travel on it caused me a lot of anxiety.

But I did what I have taught myself to do when facing anxiety. I tell myself that millions of other people do it and if they can do it so can I. And I go.

A few blocks from my hotel was the Tochomae Station and I took the Oedo Line to Roppongi. In Roppongi I found my way to the Franciscan Church for a Spiritual meeting.

Afterwards I tried finding my way around into Roppongi proper but after walking for what felt like miles, I actually wound up making a huge circle and wound up back in front of the Franciscan Church I had just left. I will never be able to figure out how that happened.

I made my way back to the hotel on the same subway line and got back just in time for the 6-8 P.M. cocktail hour, which was in a special place for people who had a certain grade room. Sort of like a V.I.P. kind of thing. It was actually a free dinner.

And btw, the breakfasts were amazing. They were held in a private lounge on a high floor with a beautiful view of Japan, and they had a chef that made you bacon and eggs, or an omelet any way you wanted.

All of the women who worked there were so accommodating and beautiful and I met Aki, Yurie, and Hinako, and now we all follow each other on Instagram.

TOKYO - DAY 4

On this day I took the challenge of going to the Shinjuku station, which is the biggest subway station in the world. I had to get my Shinkansen (bullet train) ticket in order to get to Kyoto at the end of the week.

After about an hour of being sent to different levels of the station, and believe me there are many, I finally found the Japan Rail counter on the level where I had started in the first place.

There were several people behind the counter. Mostly young girls and one old man. I got the old man. I know he was certain he was speaking English but I couldn't understand a word he said.

And this was very important. I had to make exact travel plans with a man I really didn't understand, who didn't understand me either.

I didn't want to hurt his feelings but finally I asked for a manager, who came over to try and help but also did not speak good English, but she at least had the sense to call someone on the phone who did.

It was such an ordeal that I only bought a one-way ticket and not the round trip that I really needed just to get it over with. This fact almost caused me a lot of trouble later that week.

I left there feeling very drained but did not return to my hotel room despite the fact that I wanted to get into bed. I took the subway to two different areas of Tokyo, Asakusa and Harajuku, and learned a great lesson.

I learned that when traveling on the subway, it's not enough to just ask what stop you have to get off. It's important to ask what exit to use to get to the street.

In New York City it's fairly easy to find your way to the street when you get off the subway. Not so in Japan. There are anywhere between 18-20 different exits at most stops, each one taking you to a different part of the city.

Also many of them are a few blocks walk apart. That day I was stuck underground for almost an hour until I was able to find someone who spoke enough English to guide me back to the street. (Fear)

They use what they call Suica cards, which are like our Metro cards and you tap them as you enter the turnstile to get on the train.

They have no train suicides there because they are smart enough to have gate-like solid contraptions that stay closed until the train stops in the station, so that there's no way for anyone to jump in front of a moving train. Genius! Pure genius!

It makes so much sense, which is probably why we don't do it here.

That evening I performed in a comedy show at a place called Two Dogs Tap Room. They have no real comedy clubs in Tokyo, just bar shows filled with ex-pats who speak English. Well, English with an accent! (LOL)

That's the show my new friend Tudor came to. The audience was from England, Scotland and Ireland, all English speaking countries.

When I was in New York preparing for my trip I thought I'd be performing for Japanese people. There were a couple of Japanese people in the audience who were fluent in English but not many.

I was able to find my way back to the train, which by the way stop running around 1 A.M., but then I got lost in the tunnels leading back to my hotel once I got off.

And again I was basically alone with no one to ask because late at night in Japan the subway tunnels can be pretty empty, so you're just wandering along by yourself, hoping you're going in the right direction. Very weird!

TOKYO - DAY 5

I went back to a district called Otsuka to do another show, this time at a place called Titans Craft

Beer Tap Room and Bottle Shop, upstairs off the street in a small room and I got the surprise of my life to find that I already had one fan in Japan.

After the show a young Japanese guy named Devin approached me and said he was excited to meet me, and was a fan of mine from The Black Phillip Show, a radio show I did with the late, great Patrice O'Neal up at XM Radio back in 2008.

That was before XM joined with Sirius Radio. Devin was really excited and said he never thought this would happen.

I think I was just as excited as he was and we took photos together, and he walked me to the train to make sure I got on the right one, as there were so many possible ways to go wrong.

It was raining out but because I try and plan ahead I even had a small umbrella with me, which came in very handy.

TOKYO - DAY 6

This day I had an exciting time meeting the best friend of my son-in-law Dero, a guy named Dan Curry who married a Japanese woman named Sumiko, and wound up moving to Japan only 90 days before I had the pleasure of meeting up with them.

They lived kind of close to where I was staying and we met in a beautiful park nearby, and decided to find a Starbucks where we could sit and chat for a while.

Dan thought he knew where it was and we wound up wandering in the street for about half an hour looking for it. When we finally found it, it turned out to have been right across the street from where we had originally been standing.

With Sumiko and Dan Curry in Tokyo

We had a wonderful time and Sumiko wound up doing something for me that changed the course of my trip.

A Japan Rail Pass is good for either 7 days or 14 days and when you pick it up you have to tell them what day you want it to start being activated.

I needed mine to start on Oct. 7th the day I was planning on taking the Shinkansen to Kyoto.

However one of the concierges in my hotel mis-advised me to use my Japan Rail Pass to get on one of the subway lines, the Yamanote Line, and without thinking about it I did that.

Inadvertently that action caused it to activate sooner than it was supposed to, which would not have allowed it to be active for my trip from Kyoto back to Tokyo on Oct. 14th.

When I realized that, I also realized that there was no way I could explain all that to the Japan Rail Pass people because my Japanese was too limited, and from my earlier experience with the man who was convinced he spoke English, I knew I was facing a serious problem.

I happened to mention it to Sumiko, and in her kindness, she asked her husband to pick up their daughter Marina at school so she could personally take me back to the Shinjuku Station, fight the crowds, and tell the Japan Rail Pass people of my dilemma.

She not only waited on line with me for quite a while but when we got to the ticket agent, she got them to admit that THEY had made a mistake. They erased the earlier stamp, which had activated my pass prematurely, and corrected it to go from Oct. 7th to Oct. 14th exactly when I needed it.

If it hadn't been for her I'd probably still be there trying to make myself understood. I have to say that her kindness was matched at least five times by total strangers who literally left where they were headed to physically take me to my destination.

I had heard that the Japanese people were very kind and accommodating, but I never expected it to the level that I experienced.

One time two girls who were headed to a city called Nagoya got off the train to personally escort me to my hotel, and a woman carrying a three year old child, not in a carriage but literally carrying him, took me ten minutes out of her way through a subway station, down an escalator and out a back door to guide me to another section of the city.

Unfortunately I didn't have enough Japanese to tell her that it wasn't necessary.

After that I got back on the subway and found my way to the famous Takeshita Street, the famous fashion street in the Harajuku district of Tokyo, then made my way to the Shibuya Crossing the biggest street crossing in the world.

It's hard to imagine how many thousands of people could be crossing the street at the same time. It sounds like an opportunity for The Guinness Book of Records! Come to think of it it's probably already in there.

While at that crossing I saw two Caucasian girls, one with purple hair holding a baby, and the other with pink hair, and found out it was a girl named Jen from the U.K. who had a popular internet show.

We spotted each other about the same time, and they told me they liked my hair and my look and wound up interviewing me on the street. Then I interviewed them as well for my Comedy Matters TV You Tube channel. (https://www.youtube.com/comedymatterstv)

TOKYO - DAY 7

Today I battled the trains again to go see Yanaka, the old world section of the city of Tokyo with the famous Gyokuen-In Temple and the beautiful Yanaka Cemetery, which is one of the most beautiful places I've ever seen.

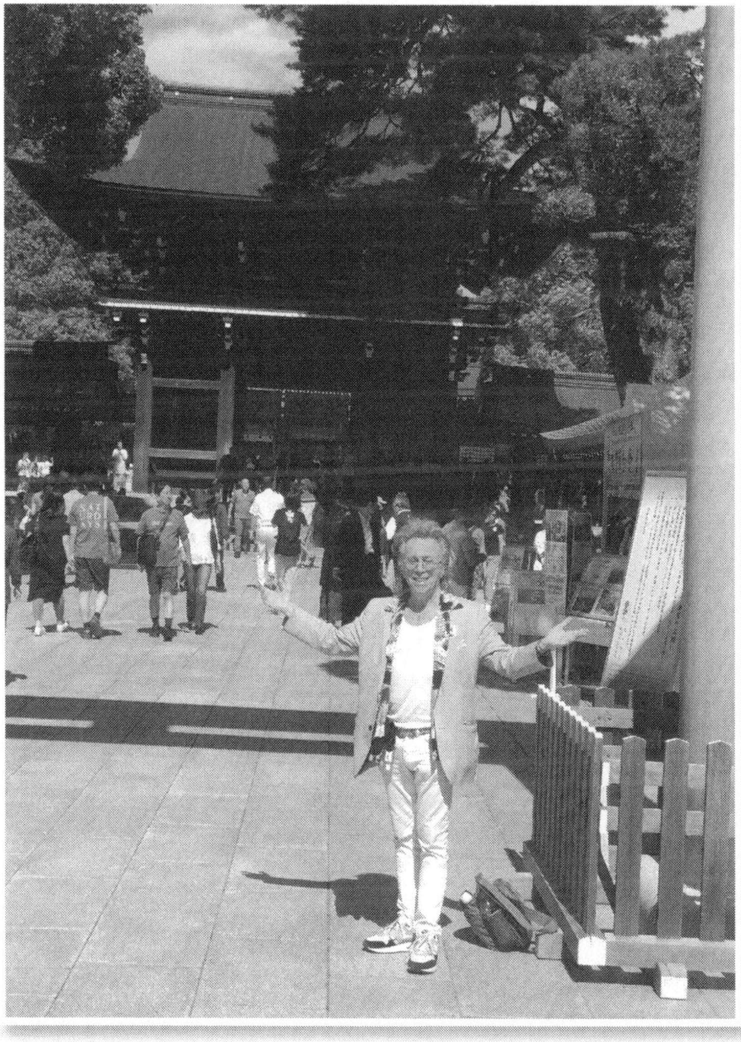

Outside of a beautiful Japanese Temple!

It's basically like a sculpture garden, and it's the place I was guided to by the woman carrying the three-year old boy.

The only thing I found strange there is that at one point a bunch of young schoolboys opened the gate and rode their bicycles through the cemetery on their way home from school. They ride through a cemetery every day like it's nothing!

Each gravesite was like a mini temple in itself with sculptures and artwork and urns and no two were the same.

I wandered around Yanaka into an area of small store fronts, food sellers, and street peddlers where I picked up some interesting gifts including a gorgeous kimono that I didn't realize was child's size until I got it back to the States.

That night my friend Kaori came by and we shot a fun video for You Tube until around 11:30 P.M. and then I packed for my last day in Tokyo.

TOKYO TO KYOTO - DAY 8

I had my last breakfast at the Hilton Hotel from their VIP area, which again is so magnificent with a view overlooking Tokyo, and then took a $40. taxi to the train station to get the Shinkansen to Kyoto.

The concierge was nice enough to write instructions for me in Japanese to give to the taxi driver and also to show the Shinkansen employees to make it clear where I was going.

I had bought a ticket for the green car which is their First Class car because I was told there wasn't a lot of room for luggage in the regular cars, and I had my usual garment bag, a big suitcase, and my carry on bag and I didn't want to have to squeeze into a potentially crowded car with all that stuff.

Once again my ADHD and my fear told me I would have trouble getting all of my luggage on the Shinkansen and I always picture myself stuck in a situation where I'm in jeopardy, or losing something important, so I battled the fear by sending my big suitcase ahead to Kyoto and trusting that it would be there when I arrived.

That was a big thing for me to do, to part with a majority of my clothing in trust that it would really get there.

Japan has a courier service that sends your luggage ahead of you so that you don't have to carry heavy luggage on trains, buses etc.

In America, and especially in New York, I would NEVER trust it to be on time, because it probably wouldn't be, and chances are good you'd probably never see it again, but Japanese people are very detail oriented which helped me make the decision to risk it.

So two days before, I had to decide which clothing I could do without for the next two days, which is very hard for me to do, then I had to pack it all into my big suitcase, and leave it with the courier desk.

For only about $20. USD they promised to deliver it to my hotel in Kyoto which was the Rihga Royale Hotel.

It's a good thing I did that because although the green car was pretty empty there would not have been room for me to have all my bags near me.

It was enough to have just the two. It was a tremendous relief psychologically, not to mention physically, to not have that third bag. I traveled much more comfortably.

For some reason the bullet train did not feel that fast to me. I took what is known as the Hikari train which was covered by my Japan Rail Pass.

There is one faster train called the Nozomi train, which every so often whizzed by us as if we were standing still.

I had brought some snacks with me for the train, but about an hour into the trip they rolled a cart through offering food and I decided to try one of those Bento boxes that contains a sushi lunch. It had Korean beef strips, rice, of course, and a little packet of potato salad.

I arrived in Kyoto, got out and searched for the South Hachijo Exit where I caught a green shuttle bus to the Righa Royale Hotel. It was very close, not like the trip to The Hilton in Tokyo.

The shuttle buses ran every fifteen minutes on the dot. And when they say on the dot they mean it. If you're not there they leave.

They also have a woman who bows to you when you get on the bus and when you get off. The bus driver also bows as you exit. It's all very polite.

Kyoto is the original capital of Japan. I think my bellman was from the original days because he spoke no English at all, which was very different from my experience at The Hilton, where all the employees spoke good English.

As soon as he left I realized I didn't know how to use the shower. It had a lot of hardware and looked very complicated.

Again my ADHD tells me I won't be able to figure it out and that I'll be unable to take a shower, and to make matters worse, that I'll embarrass myself by having to ask anyone how to use it, because theoretically I should know how to use a shower.

I called the desk and they sent someone up who spoke English and who taught me how to use it. They do not accept tips in Japan, and they actually act insulted if you try and give them one.

I had a HUGE lunch at the hotel, in a beautiful dining area with so many choices of food, you could easily gain forty pounds every meal.

Then I took an afternoon tour of Kyoto where we visited three different ancient shrines, which I love, and I got to go into lots of little stores where I finally found the colorful silk kimono-like robes I had envisioned bringing home for my daughters.

I pictured them in my mind and after much searching actually found them. And by the way, when I got to my hotel the bag I shipped wasn't there yet but there was a message that it was coming in later that day which it did. I was so glad I conquered that fear.

KYOTO - DAY 9

I had a friend living in Kyoto that I was anxious to see. It was a woman I dated that used to live in my building and who moved back to Japan some years ago. I thought it would be amazing to see her while I was in Kyoto.

Actually I couldn't picture being there without seeing her. To make that long a trip and not see her would seem insane. She was very much looking forward to seeing me as well.

I woke up this day to the news that there was a typhoon coming tomorrow. It was potentially the worst typhoon to hit Tokyo in many years. I decided not to think about it and to just try and enjoy my time in Kyoto.

Someone at the hotel told me about some sort of interesting sounding celebration in another part of the city. I got back on the subway and found my way to a part of the city where they were having an autumnal celebration.

It was cool and very crowded and I think I was the only non-Japanese person there. That never bothers me. I stayed until about 8:30 P.M. and got back in time to catch the last shuttle bus back to my hotel.

It was supposedly a short walk back to the hotel if you missed the shuttle but not knowing my way around Kyoto, and having the proclivity of always getting lost, I preferred taking the shuttle.

By the way another manifestation of my mental state, and probably a bit of OCD is that I often wake up with a song in my head that lasts literally for hours, playing over and over and over again, non-stop.

The past few days it's been the kind of song you'd hear at a skating rink, and I have no idea where it comes from but it plagues me, and as I said, it doesn't stop for hours.

Today as another manifestation of my self-sabotage I missed three shuttle buses in a row to take me from the hotel to the train station, each time forgetting something in my room that I needed to take with me.

The third time was because I thought I had lost my video camera, with all of my footage, because when I went to my room for the second time, to get a bottle of water to take with me for the day, I put my camera down and left without it, and because I spend so much of my time in fear, I didn't remember whether I had even had it with me.

So I ran through the hotel lobby like a lunatic in a panic, wondering if I had actually lost it, or just put it down somewhere, and it turned out I had put it down in my room.

Total and complete self-sabotage. You manifest your worst fears. Even if you're aware of it and can diagnose it, it still doesn't mean you won't engage in it. It's a constant battle, but you can never stop fighting. And I don't!!!

KYOTO - DAY 10

Today the typhoon hit Tokyo and I was so glad I wasn't there. Just pure luck. There was lots of damage but in Kyoto we just got a day of rain. However they said they could not send my heavy suitcase back to Tokyo on the courier service because they could not guarantee that it would get there on time because of the storm.

I tried explaining that even if they couldn't guarantee delivery in one day as they usually do, that I wasn't heading back to the States for three days, and that it was perfectly acceptable to me under the circumstances if it got there in 2 days, but they still refused to even try.

I really had to work on myself mentally to tell myself that if I had to get all three of my bags on the Shinkansen I'd figure out a way to do it.

I spent another day touring and seeing temples while looking for bargains. I got to see the legendary Sanjusangen-do Buddhist temple built in 1165 that has 1001 gold statues carved out of wood and painted gold, all of the same deity known as The Thousand Armed Kannon.

Just grasping the enormity of a project like that is almost impossible, even when you see it.

KYOTO TO OSAKA - DAY 11

It finally stopped raining in Kyoto so once again I tried convincing the courier service to send my luggage back to Tokyo but once again they turned me down.

I went and had my breakfast and thought over my options. It didn't make sense to me that a country as advanced as Japan could not figure out a way to get one piece of luggage from one place to another that was only 2 ½ hours away.

Finally in desperation I called the concierge and said that in a high tech country like Japan there must be another carrier that could get my luggage

2 ½ hours away to my next hotel back in Tokyo. Another example of advocating for myself!

The concierge said she would try and sure enough she found another company to do it. They apologized that it would cost me a whole $8. USD more but I said it was fine. They're just so polite!

They said they'd pick it up at 12 noon, so I waited from 10:15 A.M. until noon at which time they said they needed another 15-20 minutes, so I decided to put my trust once again in The Universe, and let Noriko the concierge take care of it for me, which she did.

I also decided to take one more personal challenge to myself and take the train to another city. I had been hearing a lot about Osaka and how I should definitely make it a day trip.

You could go by bullet train or you could take a subway, which would take much longer, and I decided to try my luck with the subway.

I left the hotel and found my way to a different subway line I had not used before, and traveled for about an hour to see Osaka Castle, which involved a tremendous amount of walking uphill with lots and lots of steps. Nothing in Japan seems to be built low down.

As a matter of fact I went to one place in Osaka where people used to throw themselves off of a high cliff to see if they would survive, and the very few that did thought it was some sort of blessing from the gods.

There were a few times I was so tired that I was almost ready to give up, but I didn't let myself.

At 3:45 I pushed myself to try and get to the Kaiyukan Seaquarium, the largest in the world, which was in another district and was a lot further away than I thought it was. It also was only open until around 5:30, but I thought to myself, who knows when I'll be back in Osaka again!

I had to take two different train lines, the second being the Morinomiya Line, for those of you who know, and I had a date to meet my old friend at 6:45 for dinner at the Kyoto train station. And she doesn't tolerate lateness!

I probably shouldn't have gone so far away because I created a lot of stress for myself, but I actually made it. Even after I got off the second train it wasn't easy to find the Seaquarium, but I found someone who spoke a little English and who told me to look for a huge giraffe.

Sure enough after walking for a while, I spotted a really huge giraffe statue as part of some kind of kid's attraction, and it led me right into the Seaquarium.

I didn't have long to stay but I got some great videos of huge stingrays, sharks and other interesting sea creatures, and then I left to try and find my way back to Kyoto to meet my friend.

Or at least I tried to leave but I couldn't find my way out. It was many levels down and it just kept going and going with no signs and literally no one to ask. It felt like I was back in the Sistine Chapel. Finally after much stress, I was able to find my way out.

I was told to look for the JR station and the Momoyama train, which sounded to me very much like the Morinomiya train, and I had to walk through a huge park by myself with not many signs, continuously hoping I was going in the right direction, until I finally found it.

It's amazing to me how I can picture myself walking through that park and actually feel the sensation of being there. That's how I know that my body responds to these things as if they were traumas. The fear of getting lost is so deeply engrained in my cellular memory.

By the time I found my way to the station, and took both trains I didn't get back to my hotel until about 6:20 which left me literally 25 minutes to shower, change my clothes and get ready, and race to the train station to meet my old friend.

As I entered the hotel, Noriko the concierge told me that they came for my bag and she gave me the receipt. I ran up to my room, showered, changed, jumped in a taxi and believe it or not was only a few minutes late to meet my friend Masayo.

She was waiting for me outside the train station in the street and strangely enough she could not find the Isetan restaurant she wanted to take me to, and where she had made a reservation.

I hadn't seen her in years but we recognized each other right away and she looked great. Plus, she brought me a box of delicious cookies as a present. So nice!

We finally found the restaurant and were seated. The food just kept coming out, course after course. She had ordered for us beforehand, and it was amazing.

She claimed to have a bad memory but remembered every detail of all the places we had gone in New York and all the fun things we had done together, and it was at least ten years before so I guess I had made a good impression on her. We had a lot of laughs and it was a great time.

At the end of our dinner, we parted ways and I found a taxi to take me back to the hotel. I went to bed around 11, woke up at 2 and went back to sleep until 6 A.M. at which time I had to pack to get the Shinkansen back to Tokyo at 1 P.M. to spend my last two days there at the famed Imperial Hotel.

KYOTO BACK TO TOKYO - DAY 12

Because I had gotten into the habit of going to bed so much earlier than I was used to in NYC, I woke up very early and decided to check out of the hotel early and try and get an earlier Shinkansen back to Tokyo.

I wanted to get to the Imperial Hotel sooner as it was supposed to be so special, and was very expensive besides. I wanted to get the most out of it as possible.

Hiromi, the concierge was nice enough to write out the instructions for me in Japanese, since I no longer had Sumiko to do that for me, and there would have been no way I could have explained to the ticket agent that I wanted to change my ticket and take an earlier train, with a window seat in the green car.

It was 11 A.M. when I took the hotel shuttle to the train station and the shuttle was packed, since

11 A.M. is the general check-out time and I was the very last person they let board.

They had just enough room for me and my bags. To show you how the stress of traveling affects me, just writing about it now, months later makes my hands sweat and I feel it in my stomach.

That's the power of cellular memory, so when we're trying to conquer old fears it really takes a lot of work. You can still feel the trigger but it does not have to elicit the same response.

After all these years I still experience situations that make me feel like I might stutter, which I haven't done for decades, but I refuse to allow myself to do that. It's about learning to control your mind.

So I got to the train station and gave the ticket agent the instructions in Japanese which worked like a charm. He read the Japanese very easily because he was Japanese, and put me on an 11:59 Shinkansen on Track 11, my lucky number, to get me to the Tokyo Station.

However when I got to Track 11 there was already a train there ready to leave for Tokyo and without thinking about it I got on, not realizing they are very strict in Japan about being on the right train.

I went to my assigned seat which was 1A and of course someone was sitting in it, so I grabbed 2A, and hoped that no conductor would come along. Unfortunately for me, that was not to be.

About 40 minutes into the trip a very stern conductor came through the car and asked me for my ticket. Once again I manifested my worst fears. He checked my ticket and said in a very gruff voice, "Wrong train, come with me."

And I felt like I was being arrested. I gathered all my belongings, had to take my bag down from the overhead bin, and I started following him out of the train car and into the next car. He looked very angry and I was nervous.

All he did was take me to the next car and found me a seat. That was it. I felt like I was being taken to the principal's office, but I think it was his lack of English that made him sound so stern and abrupt.

When we finally got to Tokyo station I had another note in Japanese for the taxi driver, thanks to the concierge at the Rihga Royale hotel. It was a short ride, only $6.50 USD and of course my credit card wouldn't work in his machine, but fortunately I carry an extra card because I try and think of every possible thing that can go wrong.

The Imperial Hotel knocked me out. It was gorgeous, huge, and elegant, with so many staff greeting my arrival, and everyone bowing and so polite.

I was taken to a V.I.P. floor where women in kimonos were at a reception desk where they offered you complimentary snacks and water.

With one of the beautiful kimono clad ladies who work in the hotel, and greet you with a bow when you enter.

My room was beautiful with a phenomenal bathroom, just like I like, with plenty of thick monogrammed towels, lots of amenities and the bellman talked to me for a while, in very good English.

He showed me around the room, and how everything worked. I was immediately sorry I only had two days there.

The concierge gave me instructions on how to get to Shimokitazawa, a section of the city where there was supposed to be a comedy club called Good Heavens. My friend Tom Rhodes, an international comedian told me about it and told me to look up the owner Paul Davies.

First I had to practice saying Shimokitazawa because I kept calling it Chemoshitazawa as if it was some kind of Japanese treatment for cancer.

It was a hard trip because although the concierge gave me instructions on how to get there she didn't tell me how to go once I got off the train. Sometimes when I get nervous I forget to ask all the questions I need to ask.

I left to go there around 3:30 P.M. and was so exhausted from the trip, having to take two trains that I almost gave up finding the place. But I didn't!

Just by chance I chose an interesting looking street that felt like it went on forever. I wandered along looking in every interesting store, getting more and more tired as I went.

To make it more complicated it started raining, but fortunately I had an umbrella. Everyone in Japan uses white see-through umbrellas.

The only thing I knew was that the place was above an antique clothing store called "Chicago", but I didn't have an exact address.

Just as I was about to give up for the last time, I happened to glance to my left and I saw the sign for Chicago. I couldn't believe it. It was truly by accident.

I browsed in the clothing store for a few minutes then made my way to the second floor to the sign that said "Good Heavens." I walked into what appeared to be more of a bookstore, or a library than a comedy club.

Although it was closed and kind of dark, I could see what a great room it was. A really nice woman greeted me from behind a counter, and I introduced myself as a comedy person, and said I was looking for Paul Davies.

Paul wasn't there but the woman introduced herself as his wife Hisako. I told her who I was and about my friendship with Tom Rhodes who she said was the very first headliner they had, and she told me all about the club and what days they were open for comedy.

I wound up shooting a little video with her and her employee Minami who was adorable and very sweet and helpful. She's now in the United States going to college.

When it was time for me to leave, Hisako was so kind and insisted on walking me to the subway to make sure I didn't get lost. It's amazing how many people are willing to do that, and how much stress it takes away when I have someone to guide me.

Not only did she take me, but she bought a ticket so she could actually take me to the right track. I've never experienced the level of kindness that I did in Japan.

And we all connected on Instagram, and continuously like each other's postings. It feels so weird knowing that I know people who live in Japan! (LOL)

When I got back to the hotel I had dinner upstairs in their special lounge, and I had ordered grilled chicken. After a while the waiter came back and very apologetically told me they were out of grilled chicken, so I ordered pasta bolognese which was not on the menu but they made it for me as a special order, and didn't charge me extra.

I ate part of it and asked to have the rest wrapped up. I expected a doggy bag like they do here. They said they'd send it to my room. I certainly did not expect to receive a dining table on wheels with all the settings brought to me by room service, including fresh flowers, so I could finish what was left of my meal.

I put it in the fridge to save for my last day.

TOKYO - DAY 13

I had a big breakfast in the special dining room on the 17th floor, reserved for those tenants on the higher floors. It was kind of a V.I.P restaurant. Then I sat with the concierge and planned my last trip to Roppongi.

I met a beautiful girl named Yuka in the street, told her where I was going and she insisted on walking me into the Hibiya subway station to make sure I got on the right train. She was trained as an architect, and unfortunately worked until night time so we couldn't get together. If you notice, that happens a lot! (LOL)

Later in the day I walked into Hibiya Park across from my hotel and met another beautiful girl named Luna, and she guided me to the Mitzukoshi department store, which was a nice walk, and which I'm guessing is like our Bloomingdales, where they have many employees waiting in front to greet you when you come in.

Then I went to dinner and stayed in to pack. My friend Kaori was supposed to come and spend the last night with me but was unable to do so, and I felt kind of alone, but I was able to handle it as I prepared for my last day.

TOKYO TO USA - DAY 14

Last days are always hard for me. That's when the fears of losing things, missing my bus, or something happening to keep me from getting where I need to go really kick in. It takes everything, and all of my energy for me to get past that.

They are irrational fears but it's happened to me so many times that I expect something weird to happen, and as I said earlier you tend to manifest your worst fears.

I had a big breakfast so that I would not feel hungry too soon, which is another fear, that I'll be hungry and have nothing to eat, or thirsty and have nothing to drink, or have to use the bathroom and there won't be one available, or else it will involve an awkward situation, and these fears still reside in the back of my mind.

Then there's the fear of being late, and missing my connection, which I don't think has ever happened but unexpected things ALWAYS come up at the last minute to almost make it happen, and that fear is also very powerful.

I had to get the special limo bus at 2 P.M. to arrive at Narita airport at 3:30 for a 6:30 P.M. flight for which I hoped unsuccessfully to get upgraded, as I was flying regular economy.

I got the limo bus that pulled up to the hotel, and it got me to Narita right on time, so I didn't have to worry. For once nothing weird or unpleasant happened.

To be perfectly honest I don't remember one thing about the trip home. I don't recall getting on the plane or anything about the trip back home at all. Not even like a dream. Just nothing. Like it never happened.

I distinctly remember the flight going there but not one single thing about the flight home. Absolutely nothing.

I think what happens to me is that even though I don't realize it, or feel it on a conscious level, on a sub-conscious level I must be in such a state of fear and anxiety that I go into some kind of dream state where all memory is deleted. But the point is I never let it stop me. I just go. And so should YOU!

CHAPTER

7

The Symptoms Of Fear

There are many symptoms of fear or things that are related to fear. Some or all of the ones I'm going to mention have plagued me at one time or another. As I've said before, fear is a bully and does not want you to accomplish anything or do anything meaningful with your life.

See how many of these things you can relate to. I truly hope it's not just me! (LOL)

1. Inability to gauge time—Many people are late all the time. No matter how much time they leave to get ready or how much they try to plan in advance they are consistently late.

   And it's not just for appointments to meet friends, it's getting to work on time, or getting to the airport on time to catch a flight. They are perpetually late and always running to get somewhere.

Being late all the time can signify either one of two things psychologically. The first is that you don't consider the person you are meeting important enough to be on time for. It makes it look like you don't care about them.

The other thing it could mean is that you don't care enough about yourself. It can be a sign of low self-esteem, that you think so little of yourself that you don't think it will matter if you even show up or not.

People who are always late also tend to think that they have more time than they actually do. They are not good with the concept of time. They think that an hour sounds like a lot of time to get ready, when it's really not.

I used to be late a lot in my earlier years. In order to correct that I had to train myself to work backwards, meaning that if I have to be someplace at 12 noon, I have to leave by 11, which means I have to start getting ready at 10, which really means 9:30, because I know for sure that I am going to waste a half hour of time doing something I really don't need to be doing.

I trained myself to think this way and now I am never late. I would always rather be early than late. Being late is just too stressful.

I just bring a newspaper with me or something to read so that if I get someplace early I have something to do.

Wasting time, like just standing on a line, causes me to have anxiety, but if I'm reading something I feel like I'm using my time productively, and then I don't mind the wait.

2. Procrastination—This is very tied in with the inability to gauge time. Putting off until tomorrow what you could actually do today is a great way to increase your stress, and allow yourself to feel overwhelmed. When that happens to me, and it happens very often, I have to do something I call "tricking my mind."

   When I have something to do that drains me just from thinking about it, and I think you can all relate to that, like knowing I have to put all my papers together to do my taxes, or make an uncomfortable phone call, I will continuously put it off.

But when I want to "trick my mind", as I tell myself I want to put it off, I go to my desk and actually start doing the thing I want to put off. I just grab all the papers I need and start the uncomfortable project, or just pick up the phone and dial before I can stop myself.

I do the same thing with exercising, playing the piano, studying Japanese, or doing any task where I think to myself, "I'll do it later."

While I'm thinking that, I mentally take back the power and go and start doing it right away. It's such a tremendous stress reliever. And it feels like I got the better of my subconscious fear mind.

3. Confusion—much of my confusion is caused by my ADHD condition and there are times I feel it really kicks my butt. Confusion definitely leads to fear, as it makes it very difficult to make decisions, and when I can't decide what to do it makes me very nervous.

4. Inability to take action—I've heard people say that when they become depressed they can't do something even as seemingly simple as answering the phone. Unless you have experienced this you can't imagine what it's like.

   Unfortunately I have experienced this and it's like the phone weighs a thousand pounds. You can be sitting right next to it and be listening to it ringing, and really wishing you could speak to someone because you're feeling lonely, and you still can't get yourself to move to answer it. You become frozen. Catatonic.

5. Extreme tiredness—All of these symptoms are tied together and you may feel one or all of them at the same time. Anytime you feel fear, confusion, fatigue, or any feeling that overwhelms you, you may suddenly feel exhausted as if you have to lie down, and take a nap.

   You may even suddenly fall asleep uncontrollably as if you have narcolepsy, or some kind of sleep disorder like daytime sleepiness.

6. Feelings of hopelessness—even if you've accomplished things in your life, you may feel like a failure and that you haven't accomplished anything. That's the sub-conscious part of your mind telling you that you'll never reach your goals, and the part of your mind that is like your enemy.

   This is a hard concept to grasp, but it's like that old saying, "You are your own worst enemy."

7. Fear of Failure and Fear of Success—these are almost interchangeable. Fearing that you might fail can keep you from even trying, as can the fear of success, because if you succeed, then people will expect a lot of you and you'll have to live up to your reputation, which is often hard to do, ... especially in the mind of someone who thinks like this.

   And with fear of failure, if you're too afraid to try and you never do, you never have to worry about being successful!

8. Self-Sabotage—this is one of my favorites to discuss because it's usually obvious to everyone but the person who is engaging in it.

It's completely related to "fear of failure and fear of success."

You finally get that big break, so the night before you're supposed to start or achieve your dream, you go out celebrating and get so drunk or so high that you miss the meeting, or the phone call, or the whatever you were supposed to do, that would have finalized that big break, and changed your life for the better.

Or you finally meet someone you like, so you sub-consciously ruin it by doing something sneaky that they find out about and you blow yet another potentially serious relationship that you've been wanting so badly for so long.

You're a singer, or an actor who gets the opportunity for an incredible audition, but instead of staying home to rest and prepare, you stay out all night overusing your voice, and drinking too much, and the next day you look horrible, you're not at your best performance-wise, and are definitely not prepared.

You finally score that great job you've always wanted, and then start slacking off, abusing the reimbursement policy, or taking advantage of the sick leave, and the next thing you know you get laid off, ... again!

Or you're married to someone you really love, but inside you don't feel you deserve to be happy so you screw it up by being too demanding, or starting arguments over nothing, or being judgmental and insulting eventually leading to the other partner breaking up with you.

I think you get the picture. Self-sabotage is also due to that little part of our subconscious mind that hates us for some reason and is determined to make sure that we're not happy.

It's a very hard concept to grasp, that part of your own mind is like an enemy that's working against you. But you definitely can be your own worst enemy.

And even when you accept that as fact, it's very difficult to fix. It took me many years to deal with self-sabotage and convince myself that I deserve good things and deserve to be happy, but every once in a while I wonder if it's popping up again.

And then I have to ask myself, "Why do I hate myself that much?" And that's what you should be asking YOURSELF if you think you fall into this category.

In my own case it caused me to have a bad stutter that started when I was about 6 or 7 and lasted well into my 20's and beyond. It was determined to keep me from accomplishing anything, because it's very hard to make your way in this world when you can't communicate.

Especially if you want to be a doctor, or a performer. Unfortunately for me, I wanted to do both! Talk about making your life complicated!

I realized one day that I didn't stutter when I was alone, which after thinking about it for a while, told me that there was really nothing wrong with me, because you can't have a disability based on your location. A man with a limp limps in every room of his home.

He can't go into a room alone and walk perfectly because it's a true disability. But if I could speak fine when I'm alone in a room and only stutter when I'm trying to talk to

YOU, then it means I'm really okay, and that there's really nothing wrong with me. It's all in my mind. Somehow, and for some reason I created it!

Now all I have to do is change my mind, which is not as easy as it sounds. It takes a lot of work but the important thing to know is that it's do-able. It's definitely do-able if you're willing to do the work, ... and I was!

I haven't stuttered in many years now, but the triggers are still there, which is an amazing fact. There are certain speaking situations that cause me to experience fear, but I don't allow myself to stutter. The triggers may stay forever. I just won't allow myself to have the same response to them.

If you stutter or know anyone that does, there is a lot more information about that in my best selling Amazon book on Happiness called "Healing Your Heart, By Changing Your Mind—A Spiritual and Humorous Approach To Achieving Happiness." You can get it as an e-book, a paperback or an audio book. **https://tinyurl.com/yx8h3mw7**

There's also a page on my website that is dedicated to Stuttering:

https://www.comedymatterstv.com/about/cure-for-stuttering/

9. Sadness and Depression—experiencing any one of the above-mentioned symptoms is enough to make a person feel sad, and if you're sad for long enough, Depression may be right around the corner.

   The idea is to try and keep in a positive frame of mind, through prayer, meditation, and the thought that none of us knows what tomorrow may bring.

You might be sad and depressed today, and tomorrow something absolutely amazing might happen. Think of it this way, ... every single person in your life besides your immediate family, ... there was a day before you knew them.

They were strangers, completely unknown to you. And then the very next day you meet them and they become a key figure in your life, and your life is not the same ever again.

This could be a husband, wife, girlfriend, boyfriend, or maybe a boss with a great job opportunity, or maybe someone who's not such a positive force in your life, but the point is that we're not mind readers, and we don't know what is going to happen tomorrow. We often think we're mind readers but the truth is we're not.

The point is that just because you feel a certain way today does not mean you will feel that way for the rest of your life. And just because you feel something doesn't make it real. Your feelings are certainly valid but they're not facts. Try and remember this little saying: FEELINGS ARE NOT FACTS!

CHAPTER

8

Battling Covid Pneumonia

We've already addressed the fear of sickness. The fear of losing your health is very powerful and can even lead to phobias. This fear could be from a childhood experience of being sick, having seen a parent, or someone close to you who was very sick, or even just hearing a story of someone who was very sick, which can affect very sensitive people, especially children.

Interestingly enough I'm writing this in the midst of the Covid pandemic of 2019-2020, and was lucky enough to have made it out of the hospital suffering with Covid double pneumonia. Regular pneumonia wasn't good enough for me. I had to have double pneumonia.

Ron Bennington from Sirius XM radio jokingly said that I got it early because I always like to be first at everything!

Having gone through more than one major health crisis myself at this point, I can vouch for the fact that if you don't have your health you have NOTHING! All the money, connections, or possessions in the world don't make any difference at all if you're sick.

I can also vouch for the fact that when you're sick, especially the way I was sick, you would give anything to have your health back.

This is my story.

I want to preface this whole thing with a HUGE thank you to the ambulance drivers, and the hospital staff at N.Y.U. Langone Hospital, from the transport people to the E.R. staff, and the nurses and doctors who saved me, all of whom are more brave and dedicated than I can even imagine.

There's a tendency to think that certain things won't happen to you despite the fact that you know they're happening to people all around you.

A few days before I got sick on Wed. March 11th, 2020 I was trying my best to carry on as usual and cover the comedy scene, which I've been doing for over 20 years. If I'm not performing I'm writing about it and supporting the performers.

We had already been kind of warned about congregating in large groups, and it was on my mind but on Saturday March 7th I sat with the great Ron Bennington, from The Bennington Show on Sirius XM, on the stage of the iconic comedy club The Comic Strip to tape an episode of my new Comedy Matters TV Podcast.

The Comic Strip is the club that launched the careers of Eddie Murphy, Chris Rock, Jerry Seinfeld, Adam Sandler, Ray Romano and so many more.

I had the honor of doing the book about the history of that club called "Laughing Legends" featuring an introduction by Chris Rock.

It was just the two of us, besides my crew of people and the club was empty. We spent an hour and a half just laughing and having fun. You can hear it on my Comedy Matters TV YouTube channel.

The next day on Sunday the 8th I attended a Jerry Seinfeld/Barry Sonnenfeld event at the 92nd Street Y, about Barry's new book "Call Your Mother", because I usually cover all of the Y's comedy related events. I never realized how similar their last names are!

On Tuesday the 10th I taped videos with Richie Tienken, owner and founder of The Comic Strip, with comics at New York Comedy Club like Corinne Fisher, and Harry Terjanian, and with Chris Mazzilli owner of Gotham Comedy Club for an upcoming project.

The following day, on the 11th I had been scheduled to attend a showcase at the Upright Citizens Brigade theatre in order to get my new "I'm Cool Card" and to see some of their new performers, and I recall being nervous to attend, and wrote to the woman in charge saying I might not be able to come because of fears of the virus. That show got cancelled anyway, which made my decision easier.

That afternoon I worked with my assistant on finishing the edit of my podcast with Ron Bennington, having no idea it was the last one I'd do, or how significant Ron would be in my recovery.

The episode for anyone who cares to watch, is posted on my Comedy Matters TV channel on You Tube, which is https://www.youtube.com/comedymatterstv and needless to say, Ron was hilarious!

That night there was a National Lampoon show at a place called Caveat. The show was called "Adult Sex Ed" and was produced by Gian Hunjan the Exec. VP of digital media at Lampoon, and because Gian himself invited me I wanted to show up and support, so I did.

Both he and Lampoon Pres. Evan Shapiro are great guys, and I like to support great guys.

I got there around 9:45 for a 10:30 show and used the extra time to find a local Trader Joe's and intuitively knew to stock up on certain things. I say intuitively because at the time I didn't realize how important that decision would be.

I wound up not leaving the house for the next 14 days due to the virus and needed everything I had bought to sustain me.

The lines at Trader Joe's were already very long and many shelves were already empty. Check out took a long time and people were right on top of each other. Social distancing had not become a thing yet.

Caveat had a nice size crowd despite the fact that people were already nervous to congregate, and I spent most of the show alone off to the side, but eventually went to sit with Gian and a friend of his. I think we even shook hands!

I can't begin to guess where I took the breath that breathed the virus into my body but when I got home that night I started feeling weird.

I started sneezing and coughing but didn't think much about it. I happen to be very susceptible to catching colds from people, and when I woke up the next day I didn't feel so good.

By Friday the 13th I had started to get a tickle in my throat, and when I get a cold it immediately leads to a sore throat so I started myself on a Z-Pack which I make sure to always keep in the house, because if I don't start it right away the sore throat gets really bad.

Not to sound over-dramatic, but this action may have saved my life. I wound up taking two courses of the Z-pack for the next ten days as I proceeded to get sicker and sicker.

I think the worst part was the nausea. It lasted 24/7. I wasn't sure if I had fever or not because foolishly I had what must have been one of the first thermometers ever invented. Something my great-grandmother might have used in Russia.

It was one of the old glass ones with mercury that you have to shake down before you use it. It was useless. I couldn't read it, but I assumed I had a fever because I was having night sweats where the bed was soaked with sweat and I felt cooler afterwards, but then the fever would always come right back.

I tried taking Dramamine for the nausea but nothing helped. And I couldn't throw up. Usually when you're nauseous if you throw up it makes you feel better but part of the torture was that it wouldn't let me throw up.

I kept telling myself it had to get better. Each day was a nightmare of nausea, fever, and body pain, but the nights were worse. Trying to get through each night until the light of morning came became a real struggle.

Then there were the full body chills where I couldn't stop shaking. That was a real treat too, and happened again while I was in the hospital where they had to cover me with four blankets to stop the shaking.

After about a week of this I was afraid I was re-infecting myself, but I didn't have the strength to change the sheets or pillow cases, so I threw the pillows and the clothes I had been wearing into the laundry bin, and moved to the other side of my bed.

On Friday the 20th my kids convinced me to call my doctor, which I did and he suggested that I go to an emergency room. He's at Lenox Hill hospital.

I thought to myself if I'm not better by Monday, maybe I'll go. I was afraid to go to the hospital because I thought I wouldn't come out again.

Due to my heart condition I was in a high-risk category and they always say that emergency rooms are filled with germs. Especially during the pandemic!

Somehow I managed to hang on for six more days, but the night of Wed. March 25th I was literally suicidal, and I don't say that lightly or to be dramatic. I was so beaten down, and so weak and so sick that I prayed for G-d to take me.

I hate even writing this as I'm doing it, because life is such a precious gift, but I wasn't thinking straight from being so sick for so many days.

I don't know how I made it through that night. I didn't want to go to the hospital in the middle of the night because that was just too scary, and you never know who's on duty in the middle of the night.

The next morning, after a horribly fitful night I woke up early, confused and nervous about how to handle getting to the hospital.

I didn't feel strong enough to even get dressed, but somehow I dragged myself into the shower, and picked out clothing I thought would be helpful to wear to the hospital.

I found some track pants, a T-shirt, a hoodie and a sport jacket with pockets so I could bring my wallet, with I.D., some cash etc. And believe it or not, I sprayed on cologne. I don't know who I thought I was going to meet, but I wanted to make sure I smelled good. I wasn't thinking clearly at all.

Then I realized I had to pack a bag and I didn't know what to bring so I Googled what to bring to the hospital and did my best to pack some things I thought I might need.

I took some underwear, which came in handy, a dental instrument to clean my teeth, a small flashlight, Zinc lozenges, and some other stuff that basically made no sense.

After I was there I thought about what I could have brought that would have been helpful.

I finally called 911, with a lot of trepidation, and they wanted to know my symptoms. They were already overwhelmed and not just picking up everyone who called.

By that time I was convinced I had fever, I was coughing, I had full body chills, and bright red blood was coming from my nose. I mentioned my cardiac history as well.

It was proof enough for them to send an ambulance for me. I don't recall how long it took but I think they came pretty quickly. Two of the nicest guys you could imagine brought this huge stretcher to my door. One who I think was named Jonathan took my hand and told me I was going to be okay.

That simple act of kindness meant so much to me and started me on the road to recovery. When you're that sick I think you revert to childhood where you feel like you want someone to take care of you.

He was impressed that I was able to climb up on the stretcher on my own, and said that of all the sick people he had taken so far, I had the best physical "presentation" he had seen.

His words were very comforting to me. It's amazing how much that means when you're so sick, because it sounds so simple.

They strapped me in tight and gave me a mask to wear, got me into the freight elevator and wheeled me through my lobby into the ambulance.

I requested Lenox Hill Hospital because that's where my cardiologist is, but they said it was too far and they were taking me to NYU Langone. I would have gone anywhere they wanted. I was just so weak and sick.

In retrospect it was so lucky they brought me to NYU Langone, because they were doing research on the Hydoxychloroquine drug and had it on hand, and I understand that some hospitals didn't have it.

The ride to the hospital was very bumpy in the back of the ambulance and the attendants needlessly apologized. The next thing I knew they were wheeling me in to the E.R. and asked if I felt strong enough to move to the hospital stretcher from the ambulance stretcher on my own. I did.

I was wheeled into a cubicle where I laid for the next several hours. At some point a nurse came in and started an I.V. in my wrist. It was hard to find a vein because my diastolic pressure was dropping and at one point was only 42, when normal would be around 70-80.

I literally begged for something to take away the nausea, and they finally brought me something called Zofran, a pill which worked after a while, and only for a short time.

They gave me I.V. fluids, extra strength Tylenol, and put me on oxygen and I recall going over my medical history with several different healthcare workers who dropped by.

I was laying next to a woman in the next cubicle who screamed with every exhalation. No exaggeration. Every single exhalation was a scream. It was wearing me down until I took control of my mind and tried my best to change the thought, like I wrote about in my books.

I had to step outside of myself, which was not easy, and realize how sick and scared she must have been, and that made it bearable.

At some point they came and did a chest X-ray of me in the bed and an ultra-sound of my lungs. It was then that a pulmonary specialist came and told me I had Covid Pneumonia in both lungs.

It sent a chill through my body. I knew I had the virus but I wasn't thinking double pneumonia. That was a scary word. Or two words!

They also did several nasal swabs of me and apologized beforehand for the discomfort as it feels like they're hitting your brain when they stick the swab so far up your nose.

I must emphasize that every single person there was so kind. I couldn't stop thanking them for their service and bravery in the face of such danger.

The Supreme Grace was that my breathing was still okay. I had taken those 10 days of Z-pack while I was home suffering. I really think that helped me protect my lungs.

They were actually debating on whether to send me home, but when they found out that I live alone, and with my heart condition, they said they'd try and find a room for me. I think the double pneumonia diagnosis helped them make the decision to keep me as well.

Sometime in the afternoon they said they had a room for me, and wheeled me through many corridors and several elevators to what they referred to as The Kimmel Center. Jimmy by the way, was nowhere to be found! (My only joke in this whole thing!)

It was an isolation room that had a sign outside that said "Negative Pressure." The room itself was huge and gorgeous but I was too sick to appreciate it. A nurse took off my sneakers and socks, gave me a hospital robe to put on, and covered me with blankets.

That started the process of me feeling like I was being cared for. As I said earlier, when we're so sick I think we revert to feeling like children again and we need to feel like someone is taking care of us.

She asked for my phone and plugged it in with a really long cord that I kept next to me the whole time, so I could stay connected to my daughters.

The room had huge windows with a view of the East River, a huge modern bathroom, and a TV that was the length of the entire wall on which you could control the lights, the shades, watch movies or order your meals.

The problem was that no one really knew how to use it because most of the staff were drawn from other areas of the hospital. I came to find out that these huge rooms were usually used for cancer patients but for now were turned into a Covid ward.

Once you could figure out how to use the computer on the huge TV, which I did with the help of the nursing staff, the food was amazing. I needed help strength-wise even to order food.

The nursing care however was amazing. Those poor nurses and doctors were so over worked, yet so dedicated. I thanked them all from the bottom of my heart! They were selfless, and never complained.

Once in a while I'd commiserate with a nurse that this whole thing seemed like a science fiction movie, ... except that it was real. They all agreed.

We only saw doctors like once a day but they said they were monitoring our condition from afar.

It was impossible to recognize any of the staff as they were so covered up. Only one person at a time could enter the room, and once they took off their gloves and gown they could not come back to answer any questions. You had to be ready to know what you needed, or wanted to ask at all times.

Some of them wrote their names on the plastic face shields they wore to protect themselves, so we would know who they were.

There was a remote control thing to summon a nurse and if you rang it, someone would ring back and ask you what you needed. I tried not to use it too much as I knew how over-worked everyone was.

Usually they came fairly quickly but sometimes it took a long time. I quickly learned that patience is key, ... along with gratitude.

One of the nurses helped me to order a meal, because when I got there I had already missed lunch, but they managed to get me a real meal and the food was amazing for a hospital.

There were no pillows available on my first day. They were so overwhelmed with patients they ran out of bedding, so they took this real scratchy blanket and rolled it up and put it behind me.

They thought that was the cause of the full back rash that developed and that was so bad they actually took pictures of it to show the doctors. Weeks later after I got out of the hospital they discovered that a body rash can be one of the symptoms of the virus. It took quite a while for it to go away.

On the second day they finally found me a pillow. They took out my oxygen cannula to see how I would breathe on my own and I was around 95-96%, which they thought was great, so I didn't have to use that nasal cannula anymore.

They kept on bringing me ice packs to put on my head, under my arms and on my ankles to bring down my fever and it worked. When I saw the thermometer at 98.6 I was moved to tears.

They were tears of gratitude for the dedication of the staff. They worked so hard to try and make me comfortable.

That second day they started me on the Hydroxychloroquine and Zinc. They didn't give me more Z-pack because I had already taken it for ten days. I started on double doses of the Hydroxychloroquine, two 200 mg. pills in the morning and two 200 mg. pills in the evening.

That night they told me they might have to move me to another room the next day. I was a bit anxious about that as I was feeling somewhat better, and wasn't really ready to go anywhere, but they told me they needed the room for sicker people, and that they wanted me to have physical therapy which I couldn't get where I was.

The next day after breakfast they confirmed that they were moving me. Sometime that afternoon they came to get me and asked if I was strong enough to get on another stretcher by myself, which I was. They wheeled me to another building called the Tisch Building, and this is where things got rough.

I was lined up in the hall as they looked for a nurse to be assigned to me. The transport guy assured me it wouldn't be long and he went and found one. I heard her say "Bed 4" and I realized my private room days were over.

I was the first one to be in the room and they wheeled me to a space near the window, but it was no longer a soothing water view, it seemed to be a view of the building I had just left because I could see the huge TV's through the windows.

I had brought my pillow with me just in case they didn't have any more but they did. Now I had three pillows, which was amazing. One for my head and two under my knees to help my back pain.

A few hours in they brought in my first roommate who was an elderly Chinese man who didn't speak English. At least not the first day. The second day he amazed us with some phrases he knew when he refused to take any medication and wouldn't even let the doctors examine him. But that first day he didn't seem to know his name or even where he was.

He was so sick he was coughing and choking on his own saliva as if he was strangling, and I was nervous for him and for myself as he was coughing into the air and I was in a very weakened condition. I called the nurse on his behalf several times because he wasn't able to.

Across from me was a tall Indian man who couldn't stop throwing up and the fourth roommate was an Orthodox Jewish man whose oxygen suddenly plunged from 93 to 80 and who had to be rushed to the ICU to be put on a ventilator.

The worst part was we all had to share one small bathroom. For me that was a nightmare. There is no such thing as vanity in a hospital. No one cares how you look, and no one looks that good!

We all had TV's but nobody used them because we were so sick and didn't want to impose that noise on anyone else. So we just layed there staring at the ceiling.

I was so weak I could hardly make my way to the bathroom.

But that night they told me they would probably discharge me the next day. I didn't know if I was ready and it made me nervous, but after being in this room for a day and seeing what I saw I was ready to leave.

The next day they told me they wanted to discharge me by noon, but no one ever came to give me discharge instructions or tell me what to do when I got home.

By 2 P.M. I was pleading with them to let me leave as it became intolerable, but when they brought my lunch I realized it wasn't going to happen right away.

A doctor came in and swore to me that he finalized my discharge early that morning but they were overwhelmed with things to do.

I didn't want to seem impatient at all, because they were so overwhelmed, even when I was told that my extra strength Tylenol was finally at my door, only 15 feet away yet it took more than two hours to get to me.

Getting medication in a hospital is not as easy as you would think. Everything has to be requisitioned and okayed by a physician and then the pharmacy has to release it and get it to your room. That can really feel like a long time, especially when you're waiting to feel better.

They said they would provide transportation home but weren't sure they could get me an ambulance. I was afraid to ask what the alternatives were. Finally at 3:25 an ambulance crew appeared and said I had to leave at 3:30. I never got dressed so fast in my life, and packed my bag as well.

A kind nurse, which really describes all of them, volunteered to go to the pharmacy to get my meds that I was supposed to take with me, which were the rest of my Hydroxychloroquine and Zinc Sulfate.

I got up on their stretcher and they strapped me in like a mummy. They strapped down my arms so I couldn't move them, and even covered my face, plus a big mask with a shield.

I asked them to uncover my face so it didn't look I had passed away. We all laughed at that.

There was no traffic and they got me home within a few minutes. My doorman had my keys and they let me into my apartment.

The ambulance workers who again were so kind, carried my bags in and wound up staying for about 20 minutes when they saw all the photos on my walls of the comedians they recognized.

I told them some stories until I felt too weak to continue. Six weeks later the bags I came in with were still in the exact same place where I put them down when I got home.

I didn't have the energy to move them or straighten up. I didn't even want to touch them. I think I had some kind of PTSD from the traumatic experience.

I also can't explain the weakness that I still feel as I'm writing this. I have been dragging myself from room to room. This thing is very tricky.

My doctor told me it tricks you into thinking that you feel better and a few hours later you feel not so great again. This went on for several weeks.

My cousin, my kids, a very kind neighbor, and even my super all made sure I had enough food and supplies. I never had such support in my life. Huge packages of food were left outside my door.

I even got a gift basket from the Dean of Temple University School of Dentistry, my alma mater!

What truly helped as well was the tremendous support I received from the comedy community, which has been overwhelming in a good way and very emotional for me.

My dear friend Ron Bennington and his co-host daughter Gail, announced my condition on his show on Sirius XM radio, and I literally got hundreds and hundreds of messages of support, and prayers from all over the country.

Many were from people whose names you'd be familiar with and I hope they don't mind that I'm reposting them. This is exactly what some of them wrote:

Ron Bennington kicked it off by posting on Twitter—"Our friend Jeffrey Gurian is in the hospital with Covid Pneumonia. Jeffrey is and always has been a true friend to comedy. If you're the praying type, how about sending some prayers Jeffrey's way. Get back to us soon Jeffrey, much love." Along with a mosaic of me surrounded by photos of me with everyone in the biz.

I got supportive messages from Nick Kroll, John Mulaney, Bert Kreischer, Jim Norton, Bill Burr, Colin Quinn, and the online comedy publication The Interrobang. Gad Elmaleh called me from Paris to send love and support and wishes for my speedy recovery.

Nick Kroll posted—"Get well Jeffrey. We are thinking of you and sending you all the healing vibes you send us!"

John Mulaney posted—"Jeffrey you are a good man and an absolute American original. Please be well and recover. New York City needs you. We want you back in action with your outdated flash camera!"

Bert Kreischer posted—"Thinking about you Jeffrey—get some rest and feel better!

Jim Norton posted—"Get well soon Jeffrey. No one has shown more love for comics than Jeffrey."

Bill Burr posted—"Jeff- You're a legend. One of the few, truly good people I've ever met in my life. Get well soon! Hope to see you on a red carpet this summer."

Colin Quinn posted—"Wishing a quick recovery to the legendary Jeffrey Gurian so he can get back to harassing us for bizarre interviews and pics!"

And Levity Entertainment Group sent me a beautiful gift basket filled with tasty snacks.

I share these things not out of ego, but more out of wonder, and great appreciation as I was not expecting this kind of support from people I admire so much.

I got "get well" messages almost daily from comedy club owners Richie Tienken of The Comic Strip who literally called me every day, and even offered to drive me home, despite having underlying conditions of his own, Chris Mazzilli from Gotham Comedy Club, Emilio Savone from New York Comedy Club and Noam Dworman owner of all the Comedy Cellar clubs who sent his love and said he looks forward to seeing me back at The Olive Tree cafe, which is the main hang for The Cellar crowd.

I got serious prayers from the head of production at Netflix, Jonathan Mussman, and from Paul Ronca, top guy at the Just For Laughs Festival, the biggest comedy festival in the world, who said I have a lifetime pass because the festival wouldn't be the same without me, and Bruce Hills the Pres. of Just for Laughs, as well as from Brian Volk-Weiss head of Comedy Dynamics, the exec team at Levity Live Entertainment, and radio legend Tim Sabean.

And lastly, a group of comedians headed by Corinne Fisher the co-host of the international hit podcast "Guys We F*@ked" with her comedy wife Krystyna Hutchinson, along with comedian/magician Harrison Greenbaum organized a group of NY comedians who made this get well video for me. They requested videos by posting the following:

"As some of you may know the beloved treasure of the NYC comedy community Jeffrey Gurian has Covid-19. He is very weak and is in isolation at N.Y.U. I told him we were all thinking of him and it definitely meant a lot to him to know his community was rooting for his speedy recovery.

Since he can't have visitors please film yourself on your phone, sharing your favorite comedy memory involving you and Jeffrey and we will edit it together and send it to him." This is what I received.

https://youtu.be/3uDZAi59i8c

So I think I can honestly say that comedy, and the prayers of friends, family and even people I never met before, nursed me back towards health. I'm a very big believer in the power of thought and the power of prayer.

When so many people are focusing their energy and thoughts on the same thing I believe it has an effect. It certainly did with me.

It's just sad that you have to get so sick in our world to find out how many people care about you, and how many lives you've touched in a meaningful way. That's why people have written about wanting to attend their own funeral to see how many people really cared about them.

I've always looked at comedy as a "Healing force" and they always say that laughter is the best medicine. At the time of this writing, I still have a slight cough and my head feels a little weird from time to time, but at least I feel like I'm going in the right direction.

I just finished my third course of Z-pack again because since I'm home I developed a Pleurisy-like condition, which is an inflammation of the lungs, where I had a sharp pain every time I breathed or coughed. It took a few days and fortunately it went away.

I'm also trying to sit with my feet elevated to get rid of the swelling in my lower legs that has built up, probably from sitting so much. In the last few days while writing this, they announced that this virus can also cause blood clots, which is what caused Broadway star Nick Cordero to first lose his right leg and after a fierce battle, eventually lose his life as well.

Luckily for me since I had that heart attack five years ago I've been on blood thinners ever since, which is what they're using to try and prevent people from developing clots. Who ever felt it was lucky to have had a heart attack? (LOL)

I try sitting on my terrace for a few minutes to get some air, but I wear a mask, because in my follow-up conversations with people at the hospital no one is quite sure whether you can be re-infected or not, so with my weakened immune system, and heart history I'm afraid to take any chances.

By the time you are reading this book, those questions will hopefully have been answered. And as a postscript, as I re-read this book for the third time, I'm actually feeling about 98% better.

I'm just staying put and praying for everyone to stay healthy and safe. This thing is nothing to fool around with.

And if any of this sounds like I'm complaining, I swear I'm not! I'm grateful with every cell in my body to be where I am because only a few weeks ago, I was in a very bad place.

During this pandemic quarantine, both the holidays of Easter and Passover had passed, and people were not able to go to their houses of worship to pray.

I wanted to offer the perspective that it doesn't really matter that we can't attend formal services if that's what you usually do. It's not the physical building or structure that you're in that determines your connection to your Higher Power, it's what's in your heart!

Anyway, I'm GRATEFUL beyond belief for having come this far, and for all the people that helped me.

I also want to thank the hundreds and hundreds of people, most of whom I know and some I don't, who were kind enough to take the time to send love, prayers and messages of hope.

You have no idea how much it means when you're so sick to know that you have touched people's lives in a meaningful way.

When dealing with the fear of illness, and illness itself, trying to stay positive is very important. It's not easy by any means, but it's very important to at least try.

A positive state of mind raises your level of vibration and in doing so strengthens your immune system. Negativity and stress on the other hand lowers your vibration, weakens your immune system and makes you more susceptible to illness.

New York 1 a Spectrum TV station did a story about my ordeal and how the prayers and support of the comedy community helped me to recover. The link to the story is here:

https://youtu.be/QX1Du6M21SY

I hope you find my story helpful in some way. And as a final postscript, three months later I am finally 100% back to myself, and just went to the cardiologist for a stress echocardiogram to make sure my heart muscle wasn't damaged from the virus, and it wasn't! A true Blessing!

CHAPTER

9

Fighting The Fear

THE SPIRITUAL APPROACH

Whenever I mention Spirituality I always make a point of explaining that it has nothing to do with religion. Many people equate the two but they couldn't be further apart.

You could be very religious and not at all Spiritual, and you could be very Spiritual and not at all religious.

Religion can be a wonderful thing but unfortunately it tends to divide us because it puts us into categories, and people not in our religion are automatically not in our category, and so it serves to separate us.

Spirituality brings us all together, because all it asks is that you believe in a power greater than yourself. You can call it Nature, The Universe, G-d, or whatever you like as long as you acknowledge that it isn't YOU!

The job of G-d is taken so don't bother applying!

Spirituality teaches us that Fear is the opposite of Faith. And where there is Faith there can be no Fear. Again words are easy to say, but hard to truly incorporate into your thinking. It takes a lot of work.

In the almost 25 years I've been studying Spirituality I feel that my Faith is strong, and yet I've experienced Fear many times. You'll notice I capitalize certain words in this book that ordinarily don't require a capital. I do it to emphasize the importance of the word.

I say that because sometimes I get comments from readers thinking that I made a grammatical error, who don't realize that I'm doing it on purpose.

I'm sure I experienced a certain amount of fear laying in the hospital with both the heart attack and the Covid Pneumonia, wondering what was going to happen to me, and maybe even caught myself thinking "Why me?" but the answer I was taught was "Why NOT me?"

Who ever promised me that my life was supposed to be perfect? Where was it ever written that certain things including illness were only supposed to happen to other people and not me?

That's the essence of self-centeredness. I reminded myself many times that for whatever reason this is my path, and I have to walk it and see where it takes me.

You can't only believe in certain principles when your life is going perfectly. It's when it feels like nothing is going right in your life that those principles are put to the test.

You have to not only talk the talk, you have to walk the walk. So in this last hospitalization, when they brought me to the emergency room I explained that they wheeled me into a cubicle next to a woman who screamed literally with every single exhalation.

Every time she breathed out it was a scream and it was very upsetting to say the least. As a matter of fact as sick as I was, it was driving me crazy, but I couldn't complain.

I had to flip the thought, and get out of myself for a minute in order to realize how scared she must have been, or how much pain she must have been experiencing in order to be in that state.

Those kinds of things are not easy to do by any means. It takes a lot of work until you can control your mind that way, but it's very helpful once you learn how to do it.

In my early days of Spiritual study I was riddled with fear and anxiety. As soon as I realized that I was awake, the fear crept in and my hands would get sweaty, and I'd feel it in my stomach and I'd start wondering what was going to go wrong first that day.

And it could be something as simple as just missing the elevator when I was leaving my apartment for work. That would be a bad sign.

And if I pulled my car out of the garage and the traffic light suddenly changed from green to red I might as well go back home and get into bed, because I was sure that nothing could go right that day.

Fear is very tied in with superstition and magical thinking.

But then some genius taught me something that actually worked. He said when you wake up in the morning before you do anything else like wash up, or go to the bathroom, slip to your knees and say a quick prayer which can be as simple as "Please release me from the Fear."

I did that for several months before realizing that one day I woke up without any fear. It was incredible. Someone actually told me something that worked. My whole life people always had suggestions that didn't work, and now this did.

So I learned to ask for guidance and when I feel Fear creeping in I know I'm losing my Spiritual connection for that moment, and I have to remind myself to say a quick prayer, or even The Serenity Prayer which is so powerful and goes "Grant me the serenity to accept the things I can not change, the courage to change the things I can, and the wisdom to know the difference."

That last line is the very most important line to grasp, because if I was not given the Grace, or the wisdom to figure out that there was really nothing wrong with my speech mechanism I'd still be stuttering today.

Each and every one of us has something about ourselves that we would change if we could. Some of those things are do-able and some are not. It is up to us to find the wisdom to distinguish between the two.

And that's where "Acceptance" comes into play. Acceptance is key in achieving Happiness and fighting the Fear. We MUST accept the things we can not change, or else it will make us miserable.

So in Spirituality we start our day and end our day with a prayer of Gratitude, and we ask for guidance from above.

If you have never done this I can understand if it feels mystical or way out there, but if you're not happy the way you are all you have to do is try it.

No one will see or even know. It's like when they tell you to pray for someone you hate. It sounds ridiculous, but it's not for them it's for YOU. Resentment is like you taking poison expecting the other person to die.

The great thing about praying for someone who has wronged you and that you have bad feelings for is that they have no idea that you're praying for them. Not a clue. You're praying for them in the solitude of your own home and they have no idea.

The concept is that you pray for them what you wish for yourself. So you pray that they find Happiness because if they are Happy maybe they'll be nicer to you, and then YOU'LL be Happy!

You have absolutely nothing to lose. Just try, and if you're not satisfied we'll gladly refund your misery! (LOL)

CHAPTER

10

Overcoming Real Obstacles

I've always been fascinated by people who overcome major obstacles in their lives. Obstacles that most people would be overwhelmed by. The kind of obstacles that would stop people from accomplishing anything.

Twenty years ago, I started cutting out articles from magazines and newspapers about these courageous people who when hit with these huge and often unexpected obstacles basically said to The Universe, "I'll show YOU!" You think you can stop me? Well think again."

These people were heroes to me. On my own small level I did it with stuttering. But what about the people who had something that they could NOT change and had to live with it. Those were the stories I found most inspiring.

I compiled all of these stories in a folder that I've been basically staring at for twenty years, wondering what I'm going to do with it. The stories will be written completely in my next book, but in this book I am going to share a few of them as an example of the kind of people that have always inspired me, when things felt hopeless.

These stories have all been made public in different newspapers and magazines.

Most recently during this Covid-19 crisis the New York Post wrote a remembrance of a wonderful man named Robert Samuels who succumbed to the virus. He was 83 years old, and lived half his life as a quadriplegic, paralyzed by a rare neurological disorder.

That didn't stop him from becoming an award-winning journalist and author, who lived in his own wheel-chair friendly home. He had served in the Air Force, and became a newspaper reporter that did interviews with the likes of Robert Kennedy, Pres. Harry Truman and even Martin Luther King Jr.

Then in 2011 he published a best seller called "Blue Water, White Water" about his experience being paralyzed from the dreaded Guillain-Barre syndrome.

He was very active in his community and lived with his girlfriend since 1994. They both passed away from the Covid virus only days apart after being allowed to share the same hospital room. She was 87. He never looked at his situation as an obstacle.

From 2014 Amy Purdy a double amputee performed on Dancing With The Stars. She had lost both legs from the knee down due to an infection that started out masquerading as the flu, but was really bacterial meningitis.

She was only 19 and went into septic shock and cardiac arrest, and was told she had only a 2 percent chance of survival.

After a two-week coma, and two years of dialysis due to a kidney problem she received a new kidney from her Dad, and wound up taking up snowboarding as a para-Olympic athlete.

One time while snowboarding she fell but her prosthetic legs were still attached to the snowboard and went flying down the mountain. She said at first she was embarrassed but then she laughed because she said, "It was funny."

She has also pursued acting and modeling and in 2012 appeared on the TV show The Amazing Race with her boyfriend of 12 years, who she went on to marry in 2015. She's also a motivational speaker and an author.

She's quoted as saying, "I got this second chance at life and I live it." You can't get more inspirational than that.

And in 2016 a story appeared about Micah Fowler, one of the stars of the ABC TV show "Speechless" who has Cerebral Palsy but did not let it stop him from attaining a starring role in a major TV show.

He depicts the disorder on screen and despite having some difficulty communicating he does a great job on the show. He started acting at the age of 5, even though he was already in a wheel chair and appeared on children's TV shows like Sesame Street and a film called "Labor Day."

He's an activist for employment rights for disabled people and is quoted as saying "Actors with disabilities face typecasting and a lack of auditioning opportunities, but I don't let those define me."

And he closed by saying "You control your own destiny by believing in yourself."

A couple more. In 2011 former NFL player Steve Gleason was diagnosed with ALS, more commonly known as Lou Gehrig's Disease. It's a neurodegenerative disease which is non-curable, causing the deterioration of motor nerve cells, which weakens muscles and eventually leads to paralysis.

When he got the news he and his wife Michel, who conceived their first child shortly after receiving the diagnosis went on a trip to Alaska, which started Steve on the track of doing all the things he'd wanted to do before he became too sick.

He began making home videos documenting his life, eventually allowing filmmakers to do this, leading to a documentary film called "Gleason" that came out in 2016. Even in a wheelchair, in 2013 he and his family managed to travel to Machu Picchu.

He formed a foundation named Team Gleason which helps others suffering with ALS, and to bring it up to the present, he's in a motorized chair and breathes and talks with the aid of machines, but in January of 2020, now with two children, he was honored with the Congressional Gold Medal, the highest civilian honor bestowed by Congress for his work as an advocate for people with ALS.

He was quoted as saying through a computer-generated voice, "It represents some joy, some encouragement, and some triumphs for the tens of thousands of families living with ALS, and others living with disabilities, or experiencing adversity."

And lastly, how about the story of New York based singer/song writer Chloe Temtchine, covered in the New York Post who goes on stage with a breathing tube and oxygen tank.

In 2013 Chloe who looks like a model was diagnosed with a rare disorder called Pulmonary Veno-Occlusive Disease, (PVOD) a type of pulmonary hypertension which caused her heart to enlarge to three times the normal size. Fewer than 200 cases are diagnosed per year.

It causes a constant high pressure in the heart's arteries and when she was rushed to the hospital she too was given a 2% chance of survival.

Having gotten through that she completely changed her life adopting a strict raw vegan diet, along with mild exercise.

I had the privilege of attending one of her performances and she's great. She too created a foundation and went on to become a You Tube star with more than 30,000 followers on Instagram.

And in her photo she wears her oxygen cannula, the same kind I recently had to wear while in the hospital for Covid Double Pneumonia. She has to wear it 24/7.

It's stories like these that to me define courage. It would have been very easy for any of these people to have become discouraged.

I'm sure they all had their down days, as we all do, and often keep it to ourselves, because self-pity is a very dangerous trap to fall into. It's one of the worst, self-defeating things we can indulge ourselves in.

Anytime I have engaged in self-pity The Universe puts someone right in front of me that makes me feel grateful again for what I have. I shouldn't need that reminder.

If you enjoyed reading this chapter you will absolutely love my next book called "Overcoming Obstacles—The Ultimate Book of Inspiration", which is completely made up of these kind of stories, collected over a period of 20 years.

Every time I read an inspirational story of someone overcoming great obstacles I cut it out and put it into what became a huge folder. I used my quarantine time during the Corona Virus pandemic to finally write that book, and it should be out within the next few months as part of a trilogy of motivational and inspirational books.

CHAPTER

11

The Epilogue

When people think of Chapter 11 they think of bankruptcy, but in this case it's the ending to this book. It's not any easier to end a book, anymore than it is to write a book.

What I'd like you to come away with after reading this book is to be able to examine your own life and see if Fear has been a factor in holding you back from becoming the superstar you deserve to be.

There's a statement that I carry in my pocket with me every single day, and the reason I do that is because it's the most powerful statement I have ever read, and I believe that when you carry things with you, you internalize the energy of that thing.

I call it "About Fear" and it's from a book by Marianne Williamson called "Return To Love." I use it as inspiration and in all of my work with people.

Feel free to make a copy of it and carry it with you too. I put it in all caps because every single word is so important. Here goes:

ABOUT FEAR

"OUR DEEPEST FEAR IS NOT THAT WE ARE INADEQUATE. OUR DEEPEST FEAR IS THAT WE ARE POWERFUL BEYOND MEASURE. IT IS OUR LIGHT, NOT OUR DARKNESS THAT FRIGHTENS US. WE ASK OURSELVES WHO AM I TO BE BRILLIANT, GORGEOUS, TALENTED, AND FABULOUS? ACTUALLY WHO ARE YOU NOT TO BE? YOUR PLAYING SMALL DOES NOT SERVE THE WORLD. THERE IS NOTHING ENLIGHTENED ABOUT SHRINKING SO THAT OTHERS WON'T FEEL INSECURE AROUND YOU. WE WERE BORN TO MANIFEST THE GLORY WITHIN US; IT IS IN EVERYONE. AND AS WE LET OUR OWN LIGHT SHINE, WE UNCONSCIOUSLY GIVE OTHER PEOPLE PERMISSION TO DO THE SAME. AS WE ARE LIBERATED FROM OUR OWN FEAR, OUR PRESENCE AUTOMATICALLY LIBERATES OTHERS."

I would love to know your reaction to this statement. For me it explained everything I ever went through relating to fear. I held myself back to make others feel good about themselves, not realizing that if I could live up to my potential I could be an inspiration for others, not a source of jealousy.

I was the kind of kid who would make believe I didn't know the answer in school, so the other kids wouldn't feel bad and think I thought I was smart. I wasn't worried that I would look smart. I was worried that they would think that I myself THOUGHT I was smart.

For some reason I was trying to be humble even as a child, but false humility is as bad as false pride. I don't do that anymore, or if I attempt to, I realize it now and catch myself.

I try to be the best I can be at everything I do, because I know it's okay to be successful and see your dreams come true. There's an abundance in the Universe and it's okay to participate. You are entitled to your share.

With that I wish you a fear free life. I purposely wrote "fear" with a small letter this time because by the end of this book, it doesn't seem so powerful anymore.

Please feel free to reach out to me by e-mail with any questions or comments, or to be on my mailing list for special events, at **Jeffrey@jeffreygurian.com** and please remember to check out my other book

Healing Your Heart, By Changing Your Mind—A Spiritual and Humorous Approach To Achieving Happiness available on Amazon as an e-book, a paperback and an audio book. **https://tinyurl.com/yx8h3mw7**

Until we meet again, I send you much love! FIGHT THE FEAR!!!

For more on Jeffrey, to sign up for his mailing list, and to receive a free gift please visit **https://mailchi.mp/jeffreygurian/healingyourheart**

And please subscribe to his Comedy Matters TV channel on You Tube at **https://www.youtube.com/comedymatterstv**

And on Twitter and IG he's @jeffreygurian

ACKNOWLEDGMENTS

In my first book, Healing Your Heart, By Changing Your Mind- A Spiritual and Humorous Approach To Achieving Happiness, which was really my sixth book but my first self-published book, and my first very personal book, I thanked everyone I had ever come across who I felt helped me along the way.

In this book my acknowledgements will be a lot simpler. I want to thank my parents Marjorie and Raymond Gurian who have transitioned to another plane, but raised me with a lot of love and encouraged me to achieve my goals.

They were always very proud of me, but the fear I inherited from them wound up making me a stronger person in my never ending quest to stand up to the fear.

It also led to the writing of this book, which I hope will be able to help a lot of people who fight fear on a daily basis the way I did for many years, and still do at times.

If I had grown up without fears this project would never have happened and if you help even one person you change the entire world.

Mostly I want to thank my two daughters, Elizabeth and Kathryn who through some miracle grew up with no fears at all. They are both such strong independent women, both working in the health field, and they are a constant inspiration to me.

I feel that when I fight the fear in my mind I'm doing it for them as well as for myself, so that I know I can be there for them as a Dad if they need me, no matter what. And they both know that as well.

And they have Blessed me with five grandchildren who are so amazing, all of them being raised to be strong, confident people not afraid of living life.

And that is what I wish for you, the readers of this book. A life without fear.

It's not just a dream, it's a definite possibility, and there's another Spiritual principle that addresses that, "If I can do it you can do it too!"

The essence of Spirituality, and one of the main principles is that we're all the same. We may look different and have different names but we have the same 46 chromosomes and the same parts, and if one of us can do something, then others can do it as well.

Once again, I put my e-mail on every page. Feel free to use it.

BIBLIOGRAPHY

The information in this book is a compilation of all I have read, experienced, and internalized over the years, and some of the information is intuitive.

I intend to list all the books and references I can think of that have influenced me, in no particular order. Publishers are included wherever possible.

Are You Really Too Sensitive, by Marcy Calhoun, Blue Dolphin Press

You Can Heal Your Life, by Louise Hay, Hay House

Spiritual Healing, by Dr. Stuart Grayson

Anatomy of the Spirit, by Carolyn Myss, Sounds True Publishing

Ageless Body Timeless Mind by Dr. Deepak Chopra, Harmony Books

Spiritual Solutions—Answers to Life's Greatest Challenges; by Dr. Deepak Chopra

How to Know G-d- The Soul's Journey Into the Mystery of Mysteries, by Dr. Deepak Chopra, Harmony Books

The Book of Secrets by Dr. Deepak Chopra, Harmony Books

The Power of Intention—by Dr. Wayne Dyer; Hay House

Manifest Your Destiny—The Nine Spiritual Principles for Getting Everything You Want, by Dr. Wayne Dyer; Harper Collins

Power vs. Force by Dr. David R. Hawkins; Hay House

A Return to Love by Marianne Williamson; Hay House

A Year of Miracles- Daily Devotions and Reflections by Marianne Williamson; Hay House

Daily Grace by Marianne Williamson; Hay House

The New Physics of Love and Your Power To Heal by Henry Grayson, Ph.D

Really anything ever written by Dr. Deepak Chopra, Dr. Wayne Dyer and Marianne Williamson!